# PRIME TARGETS

by

Donald S. Vogel

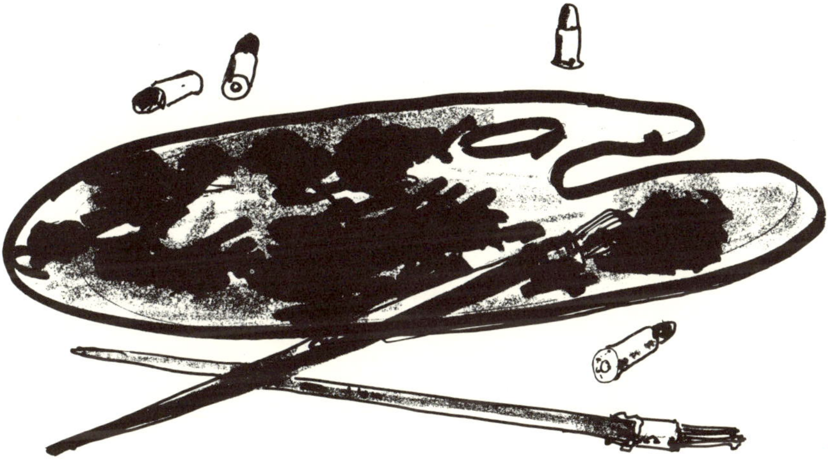

Valley House Press

Book design and illustration by author.

Typography by Defae Weaver and advisor Eric Vogel.

Edited by Billie Anastasi.


Published in the United States by Valley House Press, Dallas, Texas.

Library of Congress Number 95-9-0988
ISBN 1-879154-11-0

To my wife Erika whose gifts enhanced my life - her love and her garden —

Footprints broke the pristine surface of the snow, crossing through the back yard and the garden, around the house to the shelter of the front porch. A figure climbed the steps, pressed the bell, then stood waiting, staring blankly at the bright holiday wreath that decorated the heavy door in celebration of the yuletide.

The air was still and cold. The light, new snow blanketed the ground, its bluish tone reflecting the low-hanging gray clouds. The neighborhood was silent, the families gathered snugly indoors. Only the chimney smoke that hung lazily above each house gave evidence that neighbors were home. The houses themselves had a patina that comes with comfortable age and solicitous care. Stately trees and plantings defined the substance of the area and the success of its occupants.

It was Mrs. Forsythe who opened the front door. Her husband and daughter were playing checkers near the open fireplace in the living room. Her parents were expected to arrive later in the day, but perhaps they had decided to leave early, she thought, because of the weather. Her happy smile became a look of horror and the cheerful greetings she had prepared would not be uttered, for standing before the opened door was a nude, bearded man with dead-looking, bloodshot eyes. The scream she attempted was never heard.

***

The statisticians were busy classifying and interpreting information that would be printed as the year drew to a close. The newspapers informed their readers of the number of inches of rainfall, the number of bushels of various grains that were produced, how many Congressional bills were vetoed, and the endless statistics involved with sporting events. The editorial pages focused mainly on crime—rapes, muggings, burglaries, and of course, murder—567 murders so far, and counting, in the city.

Joe Jensen glanced through the morning paper with little interest as he sipped his coffee. His thoughts were divided between his painting and his young wife, Heather. He would ask her to sit for a portrait—no, not a formal likeness, a painting that would be personal, one that would express his deepest feelings for her. He would be casual in asking her; otherwise, she might feel the need to pose.

Heather possessed a natural beauty. It was not the kind that would make you catch your breath, but there was a quality about her that made you want to look at her again and again, and her image would linger in your mind long after she had left. She was a woman of substance. Her dark eyes sparkled; her full lips needed no added color; her smile was enhanced by her clear, lightly tanned skin. Her sex appeal was that deeply felt, to cherish and never abuse. A woman to grow old with.

She and Joe had been members of the most secret of government services, composed of an elite group of highly trained people who carry out discreet assignments in sensitive areas and must make difficult, independent decisions in the field. Heather was among its most highly rated members.

Her romance with Joe had begun when he'd requested her help finding his father's murderer and preventing the assassination of the President. It grew and matured during their second case together, when Sir Matthew Oats was attempting to take over the world's economy. After that, the President had released her from the few remaining months of her contract to go with Joe.

Heather's happy "Good morning, love!" was a welcome interruption. "May I warm your coffee?" she asked as she poured a cup for herself.

"No, thanks, maybe later with breakfast."

"So now, what have you found of interest in the paper besides more killings?"

"Unless you're interested in statistics..." he spoke while turning a page. "Hold on, here's something!" He read in silence, then said, "Listen to this—the neighborhood. Do you think its possible that...good God, I hope not."

"What, Joe? What have you found?"

"A small story, just a paragraph, an AP release from Bethesda, Maryland. 'Middle-aged couple and teenage daughter found dead in their beautiful estate home early last night by the woman's parents, who arrived to celebrate New Year's eve with them. Police were reluctant to discuss details but said that an unknown amount of money was missing from the victims' wallet and clothing.'"

They stared at each other. Finally, Heather broke the silence: "No, it can't be. How could it? Are we responsible for these poor people?"

"We'll find out." He leaned down and kissed her. "This may be a long day, so let's have a good breakfast and give some thought to it. Then we'll make some calls and if need be, we'll go to Bethesda and discreetly investigate."

Breakfast was prepared and eaten mostly in silence. It seemed so long ago that they had sealed the killer of Joe's father in the sub-basement of Jonathan Kyeth's house, they had all but forgotten him. Could it be a coincidence that the Kyeth's house was less than a block away from the scene of the murders? If not, it would mean another unwanted, and most dangerous, interruption in their lives. Jack Palmer, the killer, possessed neither morals nor conscience, and the brilliance of his mind surpassed that of any master criminal they had encountered.

Joe had tried to get into Palmer's mind, but without success, for Palmer was a vengeful man, and the very thought of revenge was repugnant to Joe. To knowingly take another's life was to diminish one's own. He had known circumstances that had created the necessity to kill, but never for revenge. It would have been so easy, at the time, for them to have killed Palmer to bring an end to his activities. But then they had arrived at a solution that seemed to provide a certainty he could never escape. If indeed he had, and that now seemed probable, Joe's happy domestic life with Heather was going to be put on hold again for some time.

Joe was six-two, built like a swimmer, lean and muscular, with brown hair and eyes. He had a good face: lightly tanned, clear skin and clean shaven. He wasn't overly handsome, but what was lacking was more than made up for by his smile and presence. He appeared to be at ease and self-assured in any company. He left the University with a bachelor's degree in English and an M.A. in art, at the top of his class. He was selective about his companions, refusing many invitations to join fraternities and political groups. The only demands he accepted were those he placed on himself. Others seemed to feel reward enough just in sharing his company.

He was awarded a fellowship that permitted two years' travel abroad for study in the arts. During this period, the die was cast. He was to be a painter which proved to be an excellent cover when he became involved in the Secret Service.

After they'd put away the last dish, Joe closed the cabinet door and turned to Heather. "I'd better call Karp," he said. "If he hasn't heard about the murders, he should be alerted to the possibility that Palmer might have escaped. With Palmer at large, the safety of the President may be in jeopardy again." Tenderly he pulled her close to him. "I was so sure that, being a painter, I could spend my time creating pleasant harmonies of color to give pleasure to my fellow men and escape their political stupidities. It looks like we may once again have to leave our shelter."

Heather kissed him and said, philosophically, "Well, you'd best call Karp to see if he knows about this and if he does he can give us the details."

Joe punched a series of numbers, waited for the second ring, then punched two more.

"Good morning, Joe. How's domestic life?"

"Domestic life is great. Love and marriage are what it's all about. I give it my highest recommendation.

"Karp, you may know why I'm calling. I just read a small AP story about a family in Bethesda..."

"Ah, yes," Karp interrupted, "the details are still coming in by fax. Want them sent on? Looks like this could be trouble. You sure you want to get involved?"

Joe hesitated a moment, then responded. "It may not be that simple. I really want no part of it. However, I feel responsible. We'll stay in the wings and observe as long as possible. If you will, fax everything to my brother, Robert, in Washington. And I suggest you try to get Frank and Darin to work undercover with the police. They need to check every house and servants' quarters in the neighborhood. H. and I will fly to D.C. in the meantime and stay at Robert's. If we're needed, we'll be available. We want to check the Kyeths house tomorrow."

"OK, Joe, I understand. We're on the same wavelength. I'll forward everything I have and let you know about Frank and Darin. Let's hope we get that bastard, Palmer, before he kills again. My love to Heather."

As Joe hung up, Heather entered. "How's our friend Karp. Was he aware of...?" Joe nodded. "I felt he would be," she said.

Joe related his conversation in full. "Looks like Palmer made it. If only I had—no, I couldn't have. So now we must live with it. The bastard, the bloody bastard! I thought we were through with all this."

Heather put her hand on his lips. "Well, look at it this way, we'll hunt him together. It's what we were trained for. If Frank and Darin join us, and Robert, well..."

"Yes, I know. But this fellow shoots from the dark. He seeks no trophies. And now I have a different and deeper concern for you."

"I understand, as I do for you, Joe. And that makes us even. Let's put such thoughts aside now, though, and call Robert. He's been writing about our past adventures, so perhaps his computer could give us a rundown on Palmer and his connections. It might turn up a few clues to give us a starting point."

"I agree. A pattern may emerge, but somehow I imagine the wily SOB will change his habits after having been incarcerated for most of two years. He's had the time to plan and plot. We have to check out the house. Perhaps we'll find some clues. Pack a few things, will you, while I call Robert to warn him we're coming. Rose will need to know that we'll be at her dinner table."

***

Robert replaced the phone and left his desk to tell Rose that Heather and Joe would be in to spend a few days. The news was most welcome, for she looked upon them as her own family. Rose had been the Jensen's cook and housekeeper long enough to rule the house with a firm and loving hand.

If it were not for her habit of wearing a simple uniform and head band she could easily pass as the boys mother. She possessed a charm and dignity welcomed in any company. Her love was felt and returned.

"Then that will make four, including your new lady friend?" Rose asked.

"Yes, four. Kathryn will be with us."

"Do Joe and Miss Heather know about her?"

"No, not yet. I'm anxious to see their response when they meet, so say nothing about her. Promise, Rose?"

She nodded. She was not about to tell, for she also wanted to enjoy their meeting.

Robert was the elder son of Ralph and Margaret Jensen. As boys, the two-year age difference between Joe and him seldom interfered with their playing together. Robert took pleasure and pride in teaching his younger brother, and he included Joe in his activities whenever possible. Both inherited physiques of athletes.

It was only after high school that their interests diverged. Robert had a bent for history and law, as had their father. Joe found a compelling magic in creating images and in the history of art. Both were exceptional students; they graduated with honors and were always on the dean's list. Joe excelled in sports, choosing those involving total reliance on the individual, such as boxing, judo, gymnastics, and tennis. He enjoyed riding and had a way with animals. After he was awarded a fellowship to study art abroad, he was secretly contacted by a man named Karp and recruited to become a member of the most secret of government services. It was a select group that worked entirely independently. Nothing was denied its members when they were working in the field. No one knew of Joe's connection with the Services until he left the group to devote his full time to painting. Not even his family had known until he became involved in pursuing the murderer of his father, Senator Ralph Jensen.

Just two years out of law school, Robert became a full partner in a major firm in the capital. It was after he had joined Joe in the pursuit of their father's killer and later, in a second adventure when they were able to squelch Matthew Oats and his megalomania, that he began to look upon his law career from a different perspective. After careful consideration, he chose to leave it to write and study art.

It was agreed that Robert would take over the family house in Washington, as it was more suitable for his occupations. Joe felt it would encourage Robert to marry and start a family. It was a happy house that held many good memories. It needed the sound of new young voices and racing feet to echo through its rooms.

During their last case, the "Transcendent Collector", they had turned the study into a communication room from which they sought to find the painted masterworks stolen from various major museums around the world. Most of the equipment was now stored in the basement, along with the files of past cases. Robert spent part of his time documenting the cases for the day when they would become novels, facts offered as fiction. He enjoyed knowing that no one would suspect their truth. Besides, economically he was immune to the politics and whims of editors and publishers.

His new-found interest in painting under Joe's tutelage would also find expression in the pages of his writings. These Robert was eager to share with his readers. In an odd way he likened himself to Dr. Watson, recording the exploits of Sherlock Holmes. Like Holmes, Joe, he felt with brotherly pride, possessed extraordinary deductive reasoning powers and the ability to anticipate and resolve problems. If pressed, Robert would admit prejudice.

As the fax machine ejected its pages, Robert read in horror the details of the killing of the good suburban family. It had to be Palmer. He was stalking them once again in perfect precision, Robert thought despairingly. The doorbell rang. Joe and Heather made good time, he said to himself. He hurried toward the door, and as he opened it, Heather pushed past Joe and offered Robert open arms and a firm kiss. He held on to her a little tighter than usual.

"What's wrong, Robert?" she asked.

Before he could answer, Joe's greeting rang out. "Big brother, how are you? Let's see, are you keeping in shape?"

"Trying to, and you—you look fit. Marriage seems to help."

"I highly recommend it. The best institution man has. And you, brother, what prospects?"

"Ah, I may have a surprise for you. Get yourselves settled and join me for coffee. I'll tell Rose you're here and wait for you in the study. Damn, it's good to have you both here!"

Joe and Heather mounted the stairs to their room as Robert headed for the kitchen with a sigh of relief. Rose was removing freshly baked blueberry muffins from the oven as he entered.

"Your timing is perfect, Rose. They're here, and we'll have coffee and your muffins in ten minutes."

"Yes, I heard them arrive. The table is already set in the breakfast room."

"Thank you, Rose. I'll be in the study till then." Robert was standing before the fax machine reading its newest offering when Joe asked from the doorway, "Much news of the Forsythe murder?"

"Too much. It must have been Parker. You'd better read these, but first we have to try Rose's fresh muffins, hot from the oven. Heather coming?"

"Here I am. I smell something wonderful coming from Rose's kitchen. Must say hello. Come on, Joe."

"Whatever it is that brought you to visit, I'm glad. We don't see you often enough." Rose's welcoming smile and voice brightened their arrival.

"Thank you, dear Rose, you bring sunshine to each of our visits," Heather said, returning her smile.

"Yes, I agree, you do that," Joe joined in. "Your muffins smell marvelous. Let's try them."

After they'd eaten the muffins and chatted a bit, Robert opened the subject of the Forsythe murders by asking, "Joe, do you think we should have killed Palmer?"

"God, what a question. Have you ever killed a man? You know my views on the value of life. I have to confess it entered my mind for a moment. But to knowingly extinguish the existence of a living being other than to save another..." he paused a moment, then added, "How can we know when..." He stopped speaking again, lost in his thoughts.

Heather broke the silence. "Well, Robert, let's see what Karp has faxed to us. Then we'll know better where to begin."

They returned to the study where Robert had neatly stacked the faxes and copies, timed and dated. The third one said that Frank and Darin had arrived and were checking the grounds at the Kyeths house. That news brought smiles to their faces. They were a full team again and would look forward to their next meeting. Frank and Darin had worked on the three previous cases. The five of them had spend enough time together on enough cases to understand each other's every nuance of movement and subtlety of expression, and to anticipate action. Whenever possible, they always kept each other fully informed.

"While H. and I study the reports, will you try to contact Frank and Darin and invite them to share dinner or to join us soon after?"

"Of course," Robert said. "I'm looking forward to seeing them. Their reports are certainly detailed."

During the next half hour, little was said. They reviewed the reports over and over. Joe closed his eyes and leaned back into his chair to concentrate on reconstructing Palmer's activities from Roberts notes he was to use in a novel one day.

A palmist at a benefit, after holding both his hands, had once told Joe, to his amusement, that he was a "new soul." When he asked what she meant, her response brought a faint, doubting smile to his face. "This," she said, " is the first time you've lived. I don't come across many new souls. Most have returned several times."

***

Joe was quite different from the rest of his clan. The family tree had brought forth many good and stable people who had pursued tilling the soil and sowing seeds, administering the law, and healing the sick. Five had served their country as officers in wartime. All were people of learning who had led fruitful lives.

Joe brought a new area of interest to the family. His early fascination with art was encouraged by his parents. The new dimension it added was looked upon with curious delight and supported indulgently, with the assumption that he would soon outgrow it.

While Joe had the physique and skill of an athlete, he was also an outstanding scholar. An eager learner, he retained all the knowledge that came his way. His gentle smile and wit attracted the friendship of both fellow students and instructors, but none could claim a true closeness with him. Only his brother Robert enjoyed that privilege. Joe belonged to no fraternity, but each group of young members had solicited his membership and been turned down went away feeling that had he decided to join any group, theirs would have been his choice over all the others.

His background permitted him to act no less than a gentleman. Foul language was foreign to his family, and seldom was it used in his presence by even the rudest or stupidest of people. There was a quality about him that prevented anyone who wanted an iota of his respect from mouthing profanities.

Joe was a thinker, a planner who enjoyed solving problems. That was one of the prerequisites for becoming a good painter. To recognize the problem would prove most important to him in both of his major pursuits, painting and solving mysteries.

He was closely watched during his last two years of college. He sensed the presence of unknown eyes, but made little of it. Being involved in the world of high crime never entered his mind until one day, a week before graduation, he was approached by the persuasive man known only as Karp.

Karp was a strange mixture. He was neither large or small, but could pass as either. By his walk, a change of expression or the slightest disguise such as a mustache, heavy eyeglasses, or a walking stick, he could change his appearance as easily as a chameleon. Karp was the man who controlled the most secret of government services. He answered only to the President himself. The members of the Services were small in number, their identities known only to him. After Joe and Heather left the Services, their friendship with Karp remained firm, and Karp continued to assist them in their cases. Now once again he would assist them with the latest in electronic equipment and exotic weapons.

Perhaps it was the exclusive nature of the group that appealed to Joe. Certainly it was more appealing than doing a stint in the armed services and having to deal with the bureaucracy of layer upon layer of officials. A significant factor in his decision was that he could pursue his interest in art at the same time. In any event, Joe felt a strong fellowship with Karp immediately. His judgment proved correct over the years. Karp was a fair, honest man whose support never wavered. Joe accepted a fellowship with the Services with the understanding of all that went with it. His cover as a traveling art student proved its worth many times in the pursuit of suspects.

Among Joe's tutors in the field were Darin Long and Frank Muller, with whom he formed an immediate and lasting friendship. Joe had worked with them on each of his adventures. The one physical likeness between the two was their age. At 46 Frank could easily have passed as a bookkeeper. Five feet eight inches tall, lean but large-boned, he was uncommonly strong and an agile gymnast. Darin was also in his late forties, six feet two inches tall, 245 pounds. Earlier he had been a professional wrestler, but for the past twelve years he had been a valued member of the exclusive Services. His bulk belied his agility, but not his appetite.

***

Joe and Heather went over the fax sheets and made notes, with the knowledge that their observations would be quite similar. It was important that they understand all the evidence found in and about the scene of the crime in Bethesda. They would wait for Frank and Darin to arrive so they could hear their observations before they opened the discussion. It would probably have to wait until after dinner, as the two were scheduled to arrive shortly.

"Robert, do you have a surprise for us?" Joe asked, observing the extra place setting at the table.

"Why do you ask?" Robert flushed a bit at the question.

"You rascal! You have! What's her name? Tell me." Joe's voice revealed his delight.

"Shh, I want this to be a surprise—if now, only to Heather. So have patience. I should have known better. That's just like a little brother!"

They laughed, and Joe said, "I understand. No more will be said. A redhead?"

"Just wait and see."

"Wait and see what?" Heather asked, as she entered the dining room. "What's so funny?" She glanced at the place settings. "Ah! Robert, you're holding back on us. A lady friend?"

Again Robert flushed. Heather chuckled. "Say no more, dear brother-in-law, your complexion tells all. Is this for real?"

"You'll just have to wait and see at dinner time," he said, laughing. "Wait and see. And no advice will be tolerated, understand?"

"Understand," Joe and Heather chimed together.

"Saved by the bells." Both the door bell and the phone rang simultaneously. "Must be Darin and Frank. Joe, catch the door, I'll get the phone," Robert said as he returned to the study.

Heather joined Joe at the front door to welcome Frank and Darin. On seeing Heather, they brushed past Joe to embrace her. "Are you still putting up with that painter? Thought you'd have enough of that brush and easel stuff by now. We can't wait much longer, you understand?" Frank said as Darin pulled him away.

"My turn to kiss the bride."

"Do I know you guys? I thought you were my friends. Well, when you're done pawing my wife, gentlemen, and I use the term loosely, come in and catch us up with your activities. We'll get to the present case after dinner. It's good to see you both."

Robert joined them. "Welcome, dear friends. It's so good to see you both again! You do look fit! Terrible business, this Forsythe affair."

"Robert, what's wrong. You look a bit disappointed. Was it your call?" Heather asked.

"Yes, my surprise guest can't make it. Her mother is arriving at the airport at seven from Paris, so we'll have to wait for another time. Oh well, it will be better for our business."

"What's this?" Darin asked. "Another Mrs. Jensen in the offing? A French lady, perhaps?"

"No, no, she's American born. But that's enough for now. I'll keep her a mystery until you meet her. How about a drink before we sit down to dinner."

As they walked into the living room, Joe touched Robert's elbow and said, "Sorry brother. I was truly looking forward to meeting your lady. We have a lot to check up on."

***

After dinner, Joe asked Frank to give a synopsis of what they had learned, since Darin was not quite finished with his second dessert. After a sip of water, Frank pushed his chair back a little, cupped his hands on his lap, half-closed his eyes as if to close out any distraction, and began.

"On December 30th, sometime during the day, Palmer rang the Forsythe's bell. We'd locked him up nude two years ago, as you recall, so he must have been gray from the cold, and bearded. When the horrified Mrs. Forsythe saw him, she was scared speechless and couldn't cry out to warn her husband, who was playing checkers with their daughter before the fireplace. Palmer strangled her immediately, broke her neck and left her on the floor where she fell. Then he was upon her husband before he was aware of what was happening. The husband received a chopping blow that smashed his larynx; his heart condition helped him die instantly. His body slumped backward. The daughter, paralyzed with fear, was helpless. Palmer broke her neck where she lay. Then he went upstairs, took a shower, cut off his beard and shaved, and rubbed himself with body oil. He took one of Forsythe's suits, underwear, shoes and socks. Then apparently he went back downstairs and ate a turkey sandwich with stuffing and cranberry sauce and a large piece of pumpkin pie. He also drank coffee.

"From the Forsythe gun collection he chose a Walton thirty-two and a box of shells. He removed all the cash in the house, which could have amounted to a little over two thousand dollars. After selecting a warm top coat and hat, he left by the front door, leaving it unlocked. He didn't take either of the two cars in the Forsythes' garage. Instead, he stole a Lincoln Town Car from a house in the next block. No one was home at the time, and the car wasn't reported missing until the following day. A clean getaway.

"You finished eating, Darin? Perhaps you should tell them about the tunnel now."

Darin stood up and walked around his chair, stretching his arms above his head. When he sat again, he leaned forward, resting his chin on a big fist. His audience smiled at his antics.

"Come, friend, get on with it, or was the second dessert too much for you?" Joe asked.

"Just trying to settle it." He belched gently. "Excuse me. Now I'm ready. Well, it was difficult to follow the footprints because of fresh snow. I had to do it at twilight with the aid of a strong beam, bending low to create a raking light. The trail led to a rusted metal door of a root cellar. The cellar was unused, perhaps long forgotten. A half metal door was found at the far end. Fresh candle drippings gave evidence that Palmer still had enough light to travel the tunnel with. I guess just enough. It was a well-constructed tunnel made of galvanized, corrugated steel tubing, five feet in diameter, with an eighteen-inch wide walkway of concrete. That is one long passageway. At its end I found the welded metal door of the sub-basement room lying on the floor and next to it the head of a sledge hammer. Life was hard during his incarceration, but somehow he retained his strength and health. Apparently, he lived largely on raw fish. The tank was all but depleted of them. It was a stinking mess. There was no writing, or no visual signs about. He's too smart for that. I can only say Palmer's a clever man, and certainly a vengeful one. I don't know whether you'd want to visit that cellar or not. Well friends, what do you think?"

"Do the police know of the tunnel?" Joe asked.

"No, they think some bum did the murders and took his old clothes with him. Frank and I volunteered nothing. The police said it was their case and they were capable of handling it without our help. They told us to beat it. We were pleased to oblige them."

"Frank, how much gas did the Lincoln have when it was taken?" Joe asked.

"A little less than a quarter tank, they think."

"How many miles per? Check it and calculate the time, get a map, and let's check gas stations within the area. He would have paid cash. You know the routine." Joe was feeling the excitement—the chase was on. "When we know his direction, we can check the railroads and airports. Darin, check police reports for the car. He may have ditched it somewhere along the line. H., you're very quiet. Any ideas or suggestions?"

"Do you think he may stay close and try a shot at us, or run, regroup and return? What would you do?"

Joe smiled at her, "I'd run far and fast before anyone could follow. If I had hidden resources, I'd claim them, rearm, enjoy a few weeks of R & R, and give a lot of thought to the question of whether or not to seek revenge. I'd relax in a nice warm, sunny place where there's little news of the outside world."

Robert leaned forward. "Joe, do you really think that's what he'll do?"

"No, not really. He's more of an animal. He needs his prey, like the male lion, who lets his mate make the kill, then takes it over. Palmer would employ assassins and stand aside and watch. But this time he may want the satisfaction of pulling the trigger himself."

H. asked, "Joe, do you think he may be trying to trick you into tracking him? He didn't know of our involvement. He only saw you for a split second when he opened the front door at Kyeths' house. You said his only words were, 'Who are you?' before he passed out. When he awoke, nude, some hours later, he was alone in the subcellar."

"I've thought about it many times, and I must give him the benefit of the doubt, even though his eyes were fixed on my hand and the dart gun," Joe said. "Even so, we've started our pursuit as of now. I can only imagine that Palmer is still on the run and recuperating from his imprisonment. It should be weeks or even months before he can mount an attack in our direction. In the past, he hired others to do his killing, and that will require time to organize. In the meantime, let's review the Kyeths affair and refresh our memories."

"I'll gather the data and his photos first thing in the morning and make copies for each of us," Robert volunteered.

"Sounds good to me," Darin agreed. "Frank and I will get onto locating the car right away. Shall we work out of this house as we did before on the Transcendent Collector case?"

"Yes, I think so." Robert said, "if Joe agrees."

"Of course," Joe nodded. "Now, let's close this and return at seven.

***

It had begun over two years ago when a letter was delivered by mistake to the Senator. On the basis of the information it contained, Senator Jensen set out to discover details of a plan by Speaker of the House Johnathan Kyeths to take over the Presidency and involve the country in a world conflict. Apparently, he learned too much and was killed by Jack Palmer, an international terrorist hired by Kyeths to carry out the plot.

The Vice President was one of the conspirators. He believed the plan was to assassinate the President and fake an assassination attempt on him while only wounding him slightly. Palmer promised to kill Kyeths for him afterwards, but the Vice President also planned to dispose of Palmer.

Kyeths' plan was to make it appear that the Vice President had killed the President. In the resultant shock and confusion, with the Vice President in custody, Kyeths would take the reins of government as President. In a chilling moment, Kyeths mused that soon he "...will have the bomb, a great many bombs, and that window of vulnerability, the period of National Mourning."

Palmer had yet another agenda. He planned to kill the President and Vice President, collect a great deal of money from Kyeths, and kill Kyeths as well. This he did by planting a bomb on the Speaker's jet, set to explode in the air as the Speaker was on his way to a speaking engagement in Dallas. Three young boys watching the plane high above them were witnesses. "The silver dot turned into a plume of white with a red-orange center... Small flashes of light, reflections of falling bits of metal debris, descended slowly toward the earth.

The Speaker, Johnathan Kyeths, had an estate on four acres of land in Bethesda, Maryland. In the attic of the three-story house was a soundproof, fully equipped "war room," where Kyeths made his plans and applied the pressures that would bring his co-conspirators fully in line with his wishes. The sub-basement of the house was secured, reinforced, and fully equipped to serve as a bomb shelter, able to sustain two people in moderate comfort for two years, or one person in spartan circumstances for as much as five years.

Joe and Heather, assisted by an old tom cat, set up a stake-out of the Speaker's house by using a tree house on the Neighboring estate. They used both very high-tech methods and their well-developed physical skills to conduct a photo and audio surveillance of the house, identifying a number of high government officials as conspirators. Joe gained access to the well-secured house to obtain computer data proving their case.

Joe's brother, Robert, was given the task of convincing the President of the plot. The President agreed to a denouement at Camp David in which Joe and two other members of the Special Services would thwart the hired Iranian assassins and bring the conspirators to justice.

Palmer, unaware that the plot had been discovered, planted another bomb on the plane the Iranian terrorists would use for their escape, and they were killed. The conspirators were rounded up, and Joe captured Palmer. Joe and one of the Service men used a dart tipped with a substance that knocked Palmer out for several hours. They stripped him and placed him in the sub-basement of Kyeths' Bethesda house, sealing the door so that he could not escape. It was believed that Palmer would never again be a threat.

***

Robert was up early. He had the gardener bring a second computer and printer up from the basement storage while he retrieved photographs of Palmer and his Iranian terrorist cohorts. All was in place by the time Joe and Heather entered the study carrying cups of freshly brewed coffee. "Good morning, brother-in-law," Heather's voice happily cheered him on what promised to be a dreary day. Snow had fallen during the night, and it seemed likely to continue through most of the day. D.C. could be beautiful under those conditions, its frantic pace calmed, the silence broken now and then by playing children who increased the population by producing snowmen.

The sideboard held coffee and Danish. No sit-down breakfast this morning—the dining room table was covered with maps. Pads and pens were laid out. A stamping of feet announced the arrival of Frank and Darin well before the doorbell rang.

"Morning all," Darin shouted, his voice echoing throughout the house.

"Good morning," Frank's more musical voice followed.

"Well, you're in good spirits this morning. Is it the snow, or the beginning of the hunt?" Heather asked as she hung up their coats and hats.

Frank rubbed his hands together. "Must be at least 20 degrees below freezing. Beautiful though—I kind of like walking in the snow. Want to make a sculpture or throw snowballs?"

"Coffee, hot coffee is what I want just now," Darin said. "If I'd known you wanted to throw snowballs, I'd have complied. We could have a great war, Heather and me against you and Joe!"

"Come friends, let's get started, we're wasting time," Joe said, holding out a cup of coffee to each of them.

"Just a thought. No real challenge," Darin said.

They sat at the table to study the maps. Robert had used a compass to mark concentric circles from the point where the Lincoln Town Car was stolen. Each member of the team took a different quadrant and began calling service stations. So far there was no police report of the car having been abandoned or even seen, but they would be notified when it was. Shortly after 10:30 Darin hung up and said matter-of-factly, "I think we have it. A Texaco station just outside of Baltimore on 95. The attendant who filled the tank remembered the driver because of his strange questions and voice, as well as his grey, sallow complexion. He asked what day it was. He didn't even know it was the last day of the year. It was as if he wanted to talk to someone about anything. When the attendant noticed the Maryland tags, he asked where the man was headed, Philly or the Big Apple. The driver said he was just going down the road a bit, nowhere special. It has to have been Palmer. Think about talking to someone for the first time after two years of silence."

"Well, we have a direction. Philadelphia, Newark, New York, what's your guess, Joe?" Darin asked.

"My guess would be New York. If I were in his shoes, I'd drive to Manhattan and leave the car in an area where it would be stripped within hours. Then I'd take a cab to La Guardia and fly to a warm climate."

Joe paused. "Yes, that's what I'd do. Frank, do you know the head of security at La Guardia? Do you think...?"

"Understand. Shall I go, or phone?"

"Phone first."

"Good as done." Frank punched a series of numbers and waited.

"Hello, Gallagher here," a gruff voice said.

"Hi, friend, this is Frank Muller."

"Frank, long, long time."

"Everything going OK for you, Gallagher?" Frank asked.

"Yes, I'm OK."

"Good. Listen, Gallagher, I have a problem you might help me with." Frank told him briefly what had happened, described Palmer, and asked him to let them know what he found as quickly as possible.

Joe leaned back. "While we wait, let's review what we know about Palmer, just what kind of a man he is. We first ran into Jack, or John, Palmer as a minor player in Munich, the Wolfton case," Joe continued. "Outwardly, he has a calm manner. Very neat and very quiet of voice. He dresses as a white-collar worker, but his hard, cold eyes give him away. We know Palmer as a snake without rattles. He strikes without warning or cause, and mere suspicion or doubt is reason enough for him to kill. He's an opportunist. His motive has always been money—lots of money. He must have at least ten or fifteen million in Swiss banks and elsewhere. Whether he'll be able to get to any of it is the question. He'll be desperate to do so.

"He talked the Speaker of the House Jonathan Kyeths into thinking he could become president by killing off the president and the vice president at the same time, making it look like a murder/suicide. Now Palmer's the only one of the conspirators left. He knows we, and not the police, will pursue him, because he knows the Kyeths affair must be kept a secret. With all of the players in the assassination attempt who enjoyed high office, it seems a miracle nothing leaked out. No one would believe Palmer about it right away, but he could start an investigation. What a nightmare that would be, having investigating reporters on our backs!

"H. suggested that Palmer might leave just enough hidden tracks to entice us to pursue him. I agree. I think he wants us to follow him. Our advantage is that he may know Heather and me, but he'll have no knowledge of Darin or Frank. This may be a cat and mouse game, so we'll have to know when to use catnip and when to use cheese. Palmer will have difficulty leaving the country without his passport and identification."

"Don't count on that for long," Darin said. "He must have connections in the underworld or in the Iranian Embassy."

"Possible. Makes sense," Joe said.

The phone rang and Robert picked it up. "Yes, he's here, just a moment. Frank, it's Gallagher."

"Frank here, Gallagher. Any luck? Hold on a moment till I find a piece of paper. O.K. Chicago, Jan. 2, Flight 602, 4:30 p.m., American. Arrived 6:57. Good. O.K. Thanks, you're a good friend." Frank hung up and turned to the group.

"Would you believe Palmer went to Chicago? What the devil does he want in Chicago? It's colder there than here." Frank looked puzzled and shrugged. Heather asked, "Shall I go to Chicago and check it out?"

"Frank, have you any connections at the Chicago airport?" Joe asked.

"No, afraid not. He would just melt into the crowd. O'Hare is a busy, complicated airport. One of us should go."

"Perhaps Darin should. His size and gentle persuasion could get results. That OK with you, Darin?" Joe asked.

"No problem. Should I follow if I get anything.?"

"Yes. Take a dart blow pipe in case you're lucky and get close enough to use it. It will pass through security at the airport without any problem. Keep in touch whenever possible," Joe suggested.

"Good. I'll pick up a few things and be off."

"Good hunting," Frank said.

"OK then, Frank, how about checking with your CIA and FBI friends to see if anyone even vaguely fitting the description of our man entered the Iranian Embassy. If not, ask them to keep an eye out for him. If possible, look at their film."

"Understand, Joe. Will you be here?"

"Off and on. Robert will hold down the fort. H. and I will visit Karp and let him know what we're up to. That agreeable with you, Robert?"

"No problem." Robert replied. "Do you think he might circle back?"

"Possibly. Anything is possible. Maybe he'd seek protection, warmth, and comfort at the embassy. They wouldn't be aware that he killed two of their prize terrorists. OK, let's beat the bushes. The hunt's on."

Joe smiled, "Good luck, and happy hunting."

***

The warehouse was on an unkempt street, where pieces of broken wooden crates, cardboard boxes, and plastic bags littered the curbs. Empty bottles that once held cheap wine leaned against grime-tinted walls. The graffiti was dominated by four-letter words and illustrations of genitals, demonstrating the extent of their authors' literacy and interest.

The blanket of new snow was unbroken by footprints. No one had passed by on either street or sidewalk since the evening before. Joe parked across the street from a large garage door that was covered with several layers of paint, deeply scarred in places, and in various stages of peeling.

"Shall I punch in?" Heather asked.

"OK." Joe replied.

Heather crossed the street and approached a metal plate at the side of the door. She pressed the third brick on each side of the plate, which then opened to reveal a panel of ten buttons. She punched in her code numbers, then closed the panel and returned to the car to wait. The street remained silent for a short while. Then abruptly the garage door opened. They drove into a large, dark room, and the door closed behind them. When it was completely down and secured, lights flooded the interior of the empty warehouse.

A familiar voice came over the loudspeaker: "Hi, Joe, Heather, long time! Come on down."

They left the car and waited as a 1/4" steel door opened to revel a smaller room containing several doors. They opened one on their right and entered an elevator large enough to hold only three people. It descended one floor below ground level. The door opened to the greeting of their friend, Karp.

"Hello, dear friends," Karp said extending both hands. After kissing H. and enjoying a hug, he said, "Sit down and tell me about your happy life. I seldom hear of pleasant things. Joe, you get us some coffee while H. and I visit."

Fifteen minutes later Karp said, "Enough, please! Any more and I'll have to find myself a wife. You make me envious. I know that something is missing in my life. Oh well, what I give up to keep our country safe! So, Joe, what are your plans to get Palmer and what are you going to do with him when you get him? I know you won't kill him, as you should." Karp looked Joe in the eye. "You should, you know. It's war, all-out war."

"I'm well aware of that. Is it a weakness, or a strength, to operate without killing?" Joe asked.

"He'd kill you, all of you, without a second thought and without remorse. He has no values, no sense of life's pleasure. He knows that being good seldom pays, but crime does. It doesn't matter to him that the payoff is only in money and he'll have to look over his shoulder for the rest of his life."

"Well, perhaps we'll turn him over to you to have him put away under high security for the criminally insane. Is that possible, my friend?"

"Let's catch him first," Karp suggested. "Tell me where you are in your pursuit at the moment."

"Happy to. What we know, as you do, is that Palmer stole a car and drove it to New York. Then Frank found out he bought a ticket and flew to Chicago, and that's about it. Darin is on his way to see if he stayed in Chicago or flew out, and if he left, where he's headed. He may have returned to D.C. to hide out in the Iranian Embassy. Is there a way...?"

Karp held up his hand. "Good idea. Hold on." He picked up a phone and pushed a series of numbers.

"Karp here. Send me the tapes for the past week, through now, on the Iranian Embassy. I know, I know. Clear it with the President, if you have to. Yes, that's all. I'll have one of my men pick them up. Just have them ready." He looked at Heather and Joe. "How do you think Palmer will disguise himself?"

Heather said, "I think we'll know him when we see him. His eyes will give him away, for one thing. For another, his ears have no lobes, and the auricle has an odd double-"U" shape that I doubt he'll be able to disguise."

"Good, damn good. We'll know what to look for. How did you spot that?"

"Just being female. We seem to be more conscious of ears because we decorate them."

"Well, what equipment do you want for your hunt, Joe?"

Joe handed Karp a list. "This should do it."

"Give me a few minutes and I'll have it put in the trunk of your car." He disappeared through a sliding door that was all but invisible.

He returned in ten minutes. "Your car is packed and ready when you are. You want me to send the film over, or do you want me to check it and keep watch?"

"If you have the time, check it. Otherwise, send it to me at the house."

"I'll look. I want to be part of the hunt, if that's agreeable."

"Welcome aboard," Joe offered his hand. Heather kissed Karp and said, "Better start looking."

***

As Darin entered the O'Hare ramp, the speakers announced that until further notice the airport was closed to all flights, arriving or departing, because of the heavy snow. He smiled to himself; he had been on the last plane to land. A murmur of angry voices grew as would-be passengers claimed chairs and storage areas for their excess luggage. The long wait ahead gave no comfort to the travelers who had checked out of hotels and taxied through blinding snow and sloppy streets to escape the Windy City. They were trapped. For how long no one could predict. Lines formed quickly at each phone bank. Darin smiled again, knowing that before long the pace would be a slow walk, and each seat would support a limp body with head nodding in drowsiness.

He stopped an officer and asked directions to the office of the head of security, but before he could get directions, he had to convince the officer nothing was wrong. After a long walk through the unhappy, milling crowd, he stood before the door of the security office. Inside, two uniformed officers stood behind a counter talking about the weather conditions. Otherwise, the room was empty. The younger of the two asked, "Can I help you, sir?" Darin held out his badge and asked to see the man in charge.

"That would be Captain Henry, Paul Henry, sir. Just a moment." He walked down a hallway and knocked on a door. Frank could hear the muffled voice of the officer: "Captain, a man from DC. wants to see you. No, I don't know what he wants." There was a pause, then the young man said, "Yes sir, I'll bring him down."

The officer returned and said, "The Captain will see you, sir. This way." Darin was led past three doors. The fourth announced in block gold leaf letters that it was the office of Captain Paul Henry. As they entered, the man behind the desk busied himself with papers, but his visitor was not impressed.

"Sorry to disturb you, Captain. I'm Darin Long. Just made it in on the last flight from DC." He held his badge just beyond reach of the Captain, making the man leave his chair before extending his hand. He wanted to feel the Captain's grip before telling him what he wanted.

"Pleased to meet you, Captain Henry," Darin said. "You can be of immense help to me. I'm tracking a killer and I need your assistance."

***

As Frank entered the lobby of the CIA building, the light snow was dwindling away. A shaft of sunlight broke through the dark clouds, creating a brilliant glare that reflected from the white-covered surfaces. It was welcomed. People who were caught in its dazzle seemed to stop to inhale deeply, as if to drink it in. Its promise seemed to raise their spirits.

At the information desk Frank flashed his badge and asked to speak to the man in charge of Embassy surveillance.

"Your name?"

"Frank Muller."

"Just a moment, please," the attendant said as he punched a series of numbers and with phone in hand, turned away from Frank. He said a few words quietly into the phone and waited. After a long pause, he turned back and asked, "Who are you with, Mister—ah—Muller?"

"Just say Karp, that should do it."

"He says the name Karp should mean something to you. Yes, sir. I'll send him up." He replaced the receiver and handed Frank a visitor's badge.

"Do you want a guide, or...?"

"Yes, give me a guide, please. It'll save time in the bloody maze."

"Yes, of course. You've been here before, I see," he said smiling.

Frank nodded. It took a full seven minutes to arrive at the office set aside to keep track of the world's embassies. His guide, a very attractive young lady, asked, "Do you want me to wait, or can you find your way out?"

"Your company would be welcome, but thank you, I'll manage. If I get lost, I'll shout 'Fire' and follow the crowd."

She smiled. "I understand," she said, and left.

A stout, balding man stepped forward as Frank closed the door behind him. "This way, Mr. Muller. Mr. Williams will see you. Please follow me." More hallways, doors, and more doors. Frank wondered how many doors hung in the building. Three, four, perhaps five thousand. He smiled at the thought of Charlie Chaplin or the Marx brothers running in and out of all these doors, perhaps being chased by Keystone Cops or foreign spies.

Mr. Williams turned out to be a tall, lean man who had played basketball in college not many years ago. He was agile and all but leapt up to greet Frank as he entered the office. "Mr. Muller, welcome. Please be seated. Would you like something to drink?"

"Thank you, no, just information," Frank said as he slumped into a soft leather chair.

"Well, anything we can give you, we will. I just talked to Karp, and we're sending some film over to him. Is that what you're after?"

"Could be, if it's the Iranian Embassy visitors."

"That's it. It's on its way. Wires crossed somehow?" Williams asked.

"Yes and no, we need an hour-to-hour film for the next several days, or until we signal a stop. Anything inside the embassy that we can review or monitor?"

"Nothing I can say about that. Perhaps if Karp asks for it..."

"Let me call him now and have him ask."

After a moment of hesitation, Williams pushed the phone toward Frank.

"Is this a direct outside line, or is it taped?" Frank asked.

"OK." Williams opened his top desk drawer and removed a second phone. "This is what you want."

"Thanks." Frank took the instrument from him and made a call. After a brief explanation of where he was and what the problem was, he handed the phone back to Williams. Williams listened a minute, acknowledged his instructions, and hung up. He seemed to look at Frank with a new respect.

"Looks like you can have the store. Anything you want. Yes, we have the Embassy bugged. Tell me what you're after, and its yours."

An hour passed before Frank left. On the way out, he stopped to visit with his lovely guide. When he left, he had her phone number and the promise of a date.

***

Robert stood looking out the window at the sunlight on the snow as he talked. "I'm sorry to hear that your mother is so sick, Kathryn. What's the prognosis? Do the doctors agree? Can I be of help in any way? Well, if anything comes up, let me know.

We missed you at dinner, and I had so wanted you to meet Heather and Joe. You were going to be my surprise. Well, soon. We've started on a new project that will be demanding timewise, and it will no doubt make getting together a bit more difficult. But we'll manage.

"The first thing is to get your mother as comfortable as possible. Yes, I understand, my dear. Just keep in touch, and remember I'm here if you need me. Yes, yes, I too." Robert hung up and stared gloomily at the phone.

The bell on the fax machine announced an incoming message and took his thoughts away from his lovely Kathryn. The fax was from Darin in Chicago: "Snowed in, airport shut down. As suspected, our man returned to DC. Will try to catch flight back on military plane."

Robert's pulse quickened. Palmer's practically in our backyard, he thought. Perhaps we should check security for the house. His thoughts focused on what he knew of Palmer and how they could capture him without losing any more lives. A deadly opponent to be sure. Palmer was a planner, and he'd had plenty of time to plan. Visions of the man laying traps everywhere were interrupted by the sound of the door and the happy, high-spirited noises Joe and Heather were making. It made him realize how much he missed Kathryn. He went to greet them and found they were covered with snow.

"Are you disguised as snowmen? " Robert asked. "Do you think it will fool Palmer?" They stopped a moment to look at each other, then burst out laughing. "We'd better take off our coats outside," Heather said. When they returned, Robert asked, "What the devil have you been up to?"

"She pushed me down, then jumped on me, and it seems we rolled about a bit. Never can tell about women. When they become passionate, well, you must suffer the consequences. Before we could get up, several people who were watching us joined in and ended up rolling about too. It was great fun, and it certainly helped brighten the day."

"How about something very hot to drink, Joe? Is Rose in the kitchen?" Heather asked. Robert nodded.

"Karp sends his best, Robert," Joe said, throwing his arm over his brother's shoulder. "He filled my list of weapons and offered anything else we might need, as well as a few tricks to secure the house. Anything from Darin?"

"A fax. He's snowed in at O'Hare. He said that Palmer returned to DC. What do you think, Joe? Another ruse?"

"No, not this time. He's here, most likely at the Iranian Embassy, enjoying their protection. We'll know soon. Karp is getting the embassy surveillance film from the CIA. It will be interesting to see what form of disguise Palmer employs. He'll know that the entrance is covered and that he'll be videotaped."

"Do you think he knows about this house?" Robert asked.

"No, not yet. But he will. Don't concern yourself too much, though. We'll put a few tricks about. It's unlikely he'll attempt anything here. We'll be on our guard anyway, so relax. We should be hearing from Frank soon. Maybe he'll have some answers."

Rose poked her head through the study door. "How many for dinner?" she asked Robert.

"Ah, just the five of us, Rose. No, wait, Darin is snowed in in Chicago unless he can get a seat on a military plane, so I don't know. Being Darin, though, he probably will. Set a place for him, just in case. Five, Rose."

"Five it will be, then." With a smile she turned and left.

Robert picked up the phone on its second ring. "Hello, yes, yes. Karp? Joe's right here. I'm doing fine. Yourself? Good, yes, here he is." He handed the phone to Joe.

"Hi!" Joe listened for some time. "That would be of great help. Can you join us for dinner? Sorry, another time, soon. Good. Thanks." Joe placed the phone in its cradle and turned to H., who was sitting quietly, deep in thought.

"He spotted Palmer entering the Embassy?" she asked.

"More than that. He's sending photos of him over by messenger, so be on the lookout. He said Pete is on his way. The redheaded boy. He'll be wearing a green cap and earmuffs that contain a transmitter. They'll be in contact with him every foot of the way."

"He is being cautious," Heather said.

"From here on in, we all will be. I just hope we can penetrate the Embassy. I suspect the CIA has an ear in it."

Heather broke in, "Not to change the subject, but when are we going to see your lady friend, Robert?"

"Soon, I hope. Her mother's in the hospital. It doesn't look too good, so she's staying near to give consent if they have to operate." Robert looked wistful, thinking of Joe and Heather in the snow. Too bad that couldn't have been Kathryn and him.

***

At ten minutes before seven, when Frank and Darin arrived, the others were in the study examining the photos Karp's runner had delivered an hour before.

"Sounds like Darin caught a ride despite the snow," Heather said. When she opened the door, they were shaking snow from their coats.

"Hi," Frank said, "Damnedest thing you ever saw. People, mostly couples, are rolling around in the snow down the street. Not kids, grown-ups. Having a hell of a time, too. Wonder who started it?"

"Would you believe, Joe and I?" H. said. "You say they're still doing it?"

"It seems that as more people come along and see what's going on, they just join in. Haven't seen so many happy people in this town since last spring. It's contagious."

"How did you two link up? Joe asked.

"Just luck. I got a ride into town with a general who had an appointment at the CIA building, and guess who was hailing a cab when we pulled up? But tell us," Darin asked, "is Palmer at the Embassy?"

"It looks that way. We've been studying photos Karp sent over from the CIA surveillance cameras. We'll see if you and Frank can spot him," Joe said as they returned to the study. Robert exchanged greetings with them, then handed them a group of photos.

"How about that? The SOB. You spot him, Frank?" Darin asked.

"Yes, pretty clever, but not enough. His coveralls are stuffed to make him look heavy. The hands are too sensitive for a working man, though, and I remember that profile too well to miss it. And as Heather suggested, the double-"U" on the ear. His shoes are out of place for a repairman, too, so all in all, I'd say he flunked disguise."

"Right on. We all found the same faults," Joe said. "Any reports on inside conversations that may help?"

"Not of value," Frank said. "Poor quality and locations. If anything of value comes from them, it'll be pure luck, or else stupidity on their part. Whoever placed the bugs—well, no matter, they'll do us no good. But I did get a make on the Embassy, a floor plan and a list of employees. Twenty-three people in all, including chauffeurs, gardeners, kitchen help, and aides. Also two long-term guests who are suspected terrorists. I have pictures of them posing as art dealers." He removed two snapshots from his inner coat pocket and handed them to Joe while he continued talking. "They spend much of their time at the auction houses in New York, Christie's and Sotheby's during the bigger sales. They're trying to get involved with the big-name collectors, but those people seldom appear. They have dealers represent them, so they won't excite other bidders. But these guys are trying nonetheless. They look harmless, but their backgrounds prove otherwise. They like bombs and knives better than guns. They both carry blades in sheaths in the backs of their coat collars. They're said to be able to kill from 20 feet."

Joe passed the photos to Heather. "Remember their faces well. I suspect we'll be seeing them."

Robert looked from one to the other. "What can we do to secure this house?"

"All taken care of, big brother. Within the hour Karp is sending two men to cover the house with sonic wave cones that will register any movement within six feet of the house in all directions. It's not a camera, but will transmit silhouette images to a special screen. Since it doesn't require a clear path, as a camera lens does, it can be hidden in the wall ivy.

"There are two ways to gain access to the basement: the cellar door and the old coal chute door. Both will be fixed to surprise any intruder."

"I hope so. I'd hate to endanger Rose or worry her."

"Don't worry, she's well able to take care of herself." Heather said reassuringly

Robert smiled, but his face expressed his doubts that his house could withstand the revenge of Palmer and his trained terrorists. After all, these were cunning men who took delight in their trade, and their trade was to kill.

***

The Embassy gave no outward sign of life. Not a single window showed light. Its usually warm stone walls looked cold and uninviting in the chill of the gray morning light, and those walls gave sanctuary to the man who had been responsible for the deaths of untold numbers of people. Having been defeated in his most ambitious quest to kill the president and vice-president, Palmer seethed, his anger barely contained. Failure doesn't come easy for such a man.

He would never forget the humiliation of being stripped nude and left unconscious in a dark room on a cold concrete floor. His last visual memory before he was locked in blackness was the face of the man whose father he had killed. That face was etched in his mind. Joe Jensen. Palmer dismissed him scornfully. Jensen was some sort of dull-witted painter. It would not be difficult to locate him. He was from New York and had a brother named Robert who was a lawyer in Washington.

Jensen and the others would be coming after him. Well, let them. He'd lead them around until he could set them up for the kill. A slow, humiliating, tortured end. They would suffer severe physical and mental pain. It comforted Palmer to envision the many ways he would perform the act. Joe Jensen, the creative artist. Palmer would show him something about creativity. But first he must transfer funds from his numbered account to another bank. He'd have a new name, passport, a driver's license, new clothes—the Embassy would fix everything. He had only to assure them that he would do a special favor for them one day.

***

Joe could sense Palmer's presence as he sat in a car across the street from the Embassy. It was the third building from the corner on the odd-numbered side of the street. The street itself was quiet. The only tracks in the snow-covered street were those his own car had made. The early snow had erased all evidence of yesterday's traffic. From the seat beside him Joe picked up a floor plan and wondered in which room Palmer was enjoying his sleep. Could there be a tunnel joining the houses on either side? They should check that out.

There would be little activity until after nine, since this was the beginning of the weekend. In this neighborhood few people started their day before eight. Joe studied every detail of the Embassy and the neighborhood. He took pictures for future reference, in case he needed to penetrate the building itself. His thoughts wandered to his wife, who should be leaving their bed about now to begin the day. Suddenly, a flash of red in the rear view mirror caught his attention. The first footprints of the day were following a young boy, who was carrying a red canvas bag. As he rounded the corner, he removed a plastic-wrapped newspaper and gently tossed it against the door of the first house. He skipped the second house and deposited his next paper at the Embassy's door. He continued down the street leaving a paper at each house on his route.

Joe focused his camera on the second house. A light appeared in a second floor window. A figure glanced out at the solitary footprints and pulled the blind, blocking out the light.

Joe noted the smoke from the chimney as it turned a dark gray for a few moments. The furnace was being stoked. They burned coal, so there would be a chute to a storage bin.

An airport shuttle bus entered the street and passed by, seeking a number well down the block. It was time to leave. The day was beginning, and Heather would soon be on her way to the kitchen. He shivered in the penetrating chill. A cup of coffee and the warmth of H. would be most welcome. As he put the car in gear and glanced one last time at the Embassy, the door opened and a small man retrieved the Saturday morning paper, then disappeared again behind the closing door.

***

It was a happy voice that carried the old tune, "Love is Everywhere," as Heather entered the kitchen.

"Good morning, Rose, where's Joe?"

"Miss Heather. I don't know, thought he was with you. He's not been in the kitchen this morning," Rose said.

"He's not in the study. I looked in on my way here. Well, the rascal slipped out on me. I must have been in a deep sleep not to have noticed."

"Notice what, H.?" Joe asked as he entered the back door. "Rose, from now on, please, as a precaution, keep this door locked."

"Joe Jensen, what do you mean by leaving and not telling me? Heather said, coming up to him. "You know better." He kissed her.

"Don't nag, H.," he teased. "You looked so... so sound asleep, I couldn't disturb you, and I thought I'd be back before you knew the difference. Did you really miss me? Think I ran out on you?"

"Oh, shut up and tell me what you were up to," she said. "I'll bet you were casing the Embassy."

"OK, you win. I had an idea and wanted to see if it had merit. There's a lot to find out about the Embassy building and the one next to it. Since this is Saturday, it won't be easy. Most offices are shut down."

"Morning, morning!" Robert's cheery voice chimed. "Sleep well? It was a good quiet night for it. Rose, are we in your way?"

"Yes. Get on out so I can get breakfast," she said good-humoredly. Are Misters Frank and Darin joining us for breakfast?"

"No, they won't. They'll be a little late," Joe said. He put his hand on Heather 's neck and gently pushed her through the door that Robert held open.

"Anything new with your lady friend's mother, Robert?" Heather asked.

"Yes, Kathryn called late last evening. The doctors will operate this morning, about now," he said, looking at his watch. "I offered to stand by with her, but she said no, she'd keep me informed."

"What do you know about her mother?" Heather asked.

"Not much. She's a writer—a travel writer of some success, I think. Independent money, just seems to enjoy moving about and recording the sights and sounds, food, that sort of thing."

"Well, give the lady our best. We look forward to meeting her," Joe said.

A fax arrived from Karp as they talked: "Embassy has double basement. Tunnel in house NE. Five people staying there."

"Well, well," Joe said, passing the fax to Heather, "odds are our man is in the second house. It's closed up, as if empty, except I caught a glimpse of someone at the window just before I left. What do you say we have a look?"

"How are we to do that without tipping our hand?" Robert asked.

"The smoke bomb/fire-truck routine." Joe smiled and winked at Heather.

"Breakfast," Rose announced.

***

Sunday morning. Joe's watch read 6:23. Frank would be delivering the Washington Post Dispatch, turning the corner that would take him past the Embassy. No one was in sight to notice that he stopped a moment and tossed two canisters between the first and second houses before he walked on to deliver the paper at the door of the Embassy. By the time he reached the end of the block, thick smoke was billowing into the street.

The high-pitched wail of a firetruck's siren soon filled the air, ceasing as the truck stopped before the second house. Four men in full gear jumped from the running boards. Plastic visors covered their faces and gas masks hung below. Two of the firemen headed for the front door; one rang the bell while the other pounded on the door, but they got no response. A third man approached the door with a large power saw. As the first two stepped aside, the saw bit into the heavy oak door as if it were paper. A wide half-circle cut the lock away. The saw was killed as the door was kicked open.

"Hello! Hello!" they shouted. "Anyone here?" They raced up the stairs, opening each door, repeating their call. The rooms showed evidence of having been occupied. Beds were unmade, open closets contained clothes, bathroom shelves contained shaving paraphernalia and lotions. But there was no evidence to prove who occupied the rooms, no wallets or passports. "Let's check the basement," one of the searchers said. They raced down the stairs to find a third fireman in the kitchen, kicking in a door. "Basement," he said, as the door splintered.

It was pitch black. "Light switch! Where's the damn switch?"

"Here it is. It doesn't work."

They removed power lights from their belts, then descended wide wooden steps until they reached the floor of the basement. Their lights circled back and forth across the floor and walls.

"Here's the exit. Looks like one of them dropped a sock as he passed through."

"Is the door bolted?" another asked.

"Yes. No cutting through this one. It'll do no good. It'll put us in Iranian territory. Let's get out before too large a crowd gathers."

When they reached the front door, they found the fire marshal talking to a man who said it was his house and he was out with his guests for an early breakfast. He thanked the marshal for the quick response and assured him that he had insurance.

As they passed, Joe said to the fire marshal, "No damage inside, nothing out of place. We'll wrap it up."

On the drive back to Robert's, Joe patted Heather on the thigh. "You make a good fireman, my love. They were just too fast for us this time."

She laughed. "It seems so. Darin, you sure destroyed one good cellar door."

"Just acting like a good fireman ought to."

"We need to find out who that fellow is who's claiming to be the owner. Anyone see where he came from?" Joe asked.

"The fire marshal said he came out of the Embassy, but the man insisted he came from the hotel down the street where he and his guests were enjoying an early breakfast. That's not possible, of course. The coffee shop doesn't open until 6:30," Heather said.

"How do we follow up?" Darin asked.

"Well, tomorrow I'll represent the city and check out the damage and look for possible arson. Maybe with luck I could run into Palmer. Also, tomorrow we should check the banks for new accounts opened with large sums transferred from out of the country. We'll have Robert do that," Joe said.

***

Joe was wearing an off-the-rack business suit, a nondescript tie, and dark brown shoes that were cracked but showed daily polishing. Heavy plastic-rimmed glasses sat loosely on the bridge of his nose. His hair was slicked down and had a razor-sharp part. He carried a clipboard that held a pad of report forms. A precision tungsten ball pen protruded from his coat's breast pocket. As he approached the house, two men were hanging a new door to replace the one the fireman had cut with his power saw.

"Pardon me," Joe said to the men, "is the owner of the house in?"

"He was a minute ago," one of the carpenters said. Joe pressed the bell and waited. After a moment he pressed again. "You sure he was in the house?"

"Yeah, we're sure," both carpenters said.

A man left the Embassy and came over.

"How the hell did he get over there? He was in the house," one carpenter said to the other.

"What do you want?" the man asked Joe.

"Hello, sir. This your house? I'm Neil Profit, city adjuster. Here's my card, sir. I have to ask you about the alarm yesterday. If I may have a moment of your time to fill out this report, Mr...? I seem to have only an address. You are...?"

"Is this necessary? I have no complaints. It was all a mistake. Nothing I can't take care of." His eyes narrowed and expressed a distrust as his facial muscles tightened, stretching dark stained skin. A small gold ring vibrated from the lobe of his left ear in response to his quivering jaw muscles. Jet black hair in tight curls glistened from a lightly perfumed oil. His voice failed in attempting to be authoritative. He was more accustomed to taking orders than giving them.

"Please have patience with me, sir. The city insists, Mr...? I need your name for the form, sir. Is this is your house? I noticed you came from the Embassy." The man flushed. "Just visiting a friend."

Joe's tone altered abruptly. "I asked you your name." It was that change and the desire to avoid further questions about the Embassy that finally brought the reply.

"Omar Omen. I'm an investor. What do you need to know? Let's get it over with."

"Thank you, Mr. Omen. Let's make this easy and we'll be done very soon. May we go inside and sit down?"

"Yes, of course, come in."

"After you, sir," Joe said.

As they passed by the carpenters, one of them shook his head and muttered, "How did he do it?"

"Mr. Profit, you said."

"Yes, that's right," Joe nodded.

"Well, please ask your questions, and I'll do my best to answer them for you. But I must say that I have no idea where all the smoke came from. I see your firemen found nothing in the basement—did they?"

"No, apparently not. They reported having to break down the door to get in. It was bolted from the inside. That seemed odd. Is there another way out?" Omar Omen looked uncomfortable. "I, ah—, I don't think so. Ah, damn it, I don't understand. I have no answer how. It makes no sense to me. It has to remain a mystery. I'll ask the maid when she comes in."

"What's her name?"

"Hell, ah—Mary, that's it! I don't know her last name. Never did, just Mary," Omen almost shouted. "Have her call me." Joe spoke in a calm voice. This man was beginning to hate him and was looking around to escape.

"Just a few more questions to check off, sir. "First, do you agree not to hold the fire department or the city responsible in any way for what happened? Second, are you willing to pay the cost—six hundred dollars—for answering the false alarm? If you agree, please sign where I have placed the 'x'. If not, I must check the house thoroughly and write a lengthy report. You understand?"

"Yes, yes, happy to sign."

Joe handed him the clipboard and his pen. As Omen signed, Joe said, "I understand you had five house guests. Are they available?"

"No, they've gone and won't be back." He avoided Joe's eyes as he returned the pen and clipboard. "Now please go, Mr. Profit. I have things to attend to."

As Joe was about to step through the door, he stopped. "I guess you wouldn't want to give me the names of your guests? No, I thought not. Thank you again for your help."

***

"Well Robert, any luck with the banks?" Joe asked.

"We got it, after a few minor threats. Anything from the government scares them into compliance with all sorts of things. $900,000 was transferred from Zurich to a James Chapman, in the Zuka Capital Bank, a Japanese-controlled corporation out of Tokyo. It's being audited at this time, but they asked us not to tell. Their reputation, you know. Ah, what a rep!"

Joe sat at a desk and drew as he talked with Robert. Heather appeared. "Hi, love, how was the interview?" "Omar Omen, he calls himself. I left him a worried man. Here's what he looks like." Joe handed Heather the drawing he had been working on.

"Very good. Shall I fax it to Karp?"

"Please. Maybe he'll find something on him."

"Let me see it first," Robert said. "Hey, I know this fellow, I mean, ah, in court. That's it. About a year ago, but I don't remember that Omen was his name. Well, Karp will most likely know if he's anybody. I'll send it on."

"Well, Joe, what did you find out from him?"

"H., he's tied in with the Embassy, and the tunnel is in constant use. He came from the Embassy to meet me at the front door where I was talking to a couple of carpenters. They knew he'd gone into the house and were surprised when he came across from the Embassy. His guests are back in their rooms now. I caught a glimpse of one checking me out. Omen told me they'd left. It shook him up when I asked for their names, which he was not about to volunteer, of course. I did enjoy my visit. We should have smoked them out of both houses. I must give some thought to that. Any word from Darin or Frank?"

***

Awad Rashid was as close to the Ambassador as anyone could be. He was privy to all that transpired within the Embassy. No movement went unnoticed. Rashid was a quiet man who seldom spoke unless asked a direct question. He would be the one to take over if some unforeseen event immobilized the Ambassador. His position was well known to the US. State Department. He was the one member of the legation who enjoyed taking a walk each day after lunch.

This particular day he was startled when a figure caught up, then kept pace with him for more than a block without saying a word. Finally, the newcomer said, "Is Jack Palmer, now James Chapman, still with you?" Rashid didn't reply. As they reached the middle of the next block, the newcomer said, "Are you aware that Palmer killed two of your agents two years ago?"

They continued walking in silence. At the end of the block, as they turned left, the newcomer said, "Did you arrange the passport and $900,000 exchange for him? He's using you, you know. If he has left, just nod and I'll leave you. Understand?" When they arrived at the end of the block, they paused. Rashid nodded once, then turned the corner. Never once had he looked at the newcomer. Frank crossed the street and continued straight ahead.

***

"Well, where does that leave us?" Robert asked. "Our bird has flown the coop." The five of them sat before the fireplace in silence, each thinking what should be done next. Darin wondered just when Palmer had left. Frank was waiting for the phone to respond to their inquiry to the airline. Heather, her eyes half closed, looked into the glowing coals and wondered what was passing through Palmer's mind. Joe, slumped in his chair, his legs stretched out, and wiggled his feet slowly back and forth. He spoke to himself, "London to Paris to southern France, the Riveria to Provence. I remember the mention of a small 17th century farmhouse—where in Provence? Where, where?"

The phone interrupted their thoughts. Darin picked it up. "Yes. Yes, give it to me." After a long pause he said, "Thank you very much."

"Well, well," Darin said. "It's London. He arrived in London two hours ago and immediately bought a ticket for Paris."

"Ah! His next stop will be..." Joe was interrupted by the shattering of glass as a stone crashed through the window and bounced to a halt behind Heather's chair.

Frank was at the window within seconds, and Joe was out the front door in time to see a young man hurl himself into the rear seat of a shiny black limousine that carried an Embassy tag. When he returned, Joe found Heather removing rubber bands that had held a piece of tinted paper to the rock.

She handed the crumpled paper to Joe, who slowly spread it flat and read the printed block letters: "I HAVE NOT FORGOTTEN YOU, MR. JENSEN."

"We now know that Palmer knows where I am. I'm his target. Apparently he's not concerned about any of you."

"Did you see who threw the stone, Joe?" Heather asked.

"Just his backside, a youngish man, wearing tennis shoes with red soles and a heavy blue band around the top. He was jumping into the rear seat of the Embassy's limo."

"Do you think Palmer knows we know he's fled the country?" Robert asked Joe.

"Not sure. The message was to have us think otherwise, or at least put us on guard. Obviously he wanted to send more of a message than what he printed. I suspect he thinks that I'm just a painter who got in his way. I don't think he'd try such a scare tactic otherwise, throwing a message through the window. Employing a young man to do it was just dumb."

"Shall we pick up Tennis Shoes and question him?" Darin asked Joe.

"Not yet. Let's see if we can spot him on the surveillance film and check him out, background and such—you know, training to be a terrorist. He may just be a flunky hired to do this one job. Let me know what we have on him. He could be useful."

Robert said, "I'd better call the glass company and have the window replaced as soon as possible."

"I suggest you order the new extra-strength thermopane glass. It would have stopped that stone.

You'll have to give them the exact size of the window, because they'll have to make it up in their plant. Here, I'll help you measure." Heather said.

They all looked at her in awe. Joe shrugged. "That's my girl," he said.

Robert made the call.

***

An hour later Rose entered the study to announce that a man from the glass company was at the front door. "So soon?" Robert said.

"Too soon. Something's wrong. Joe, stay put. Frank, follow my lead. We'll check him out." Heather's eyes sparkled as she gave the orders.

She opened the door to find a young man holding a tool box. He was wearing green coveralls, a baseball cap and tennis shoes with a heavy blue band around the tops. He was clean-shaven and neat in appearance. "I have the glass for your window, ma'am," he said. He had a heavy accent.

"Good! Glad you made it so soon. Before you start, though, I want you to look at a cracked window glass in the kitchen. This gentleman will show you. Leave your tool box on the porch. It will be safe."

The man looked a little flustered, but complied. He seemed reluctant to leave his tools, but Frank's voice helped reassure him. "This way. What's your name?" "Jim, just call me Jim, sir."

"Good enough. This way Jim. You play baseball?" "I used to play in school."

"What school did you go to?"

As they disappeared into the house, Heather stepped out on the porch and bent over to examine the tool box. It was obvious that the panel of glass strapped to the support was neither the size they had ordered nor thermopane. The box held a machine pistol under a neatly folded rag. She quickly made a few adjustments to its mechanism and replaced it under the rag. As she stepped back inside the house, she heard Frank say, "Well, perhaps you can return tomorrow and replace it, Jim."

"That glass seems quite large," Heather remarked.

"Will you need help? Frank, ask Mr. Jensen to come help Jim."

"Yes ma'am," Frank said as he swept his open hand aside. That told Heather that Jim was clean of body weapons. When Frank left the room, Heather told the young man to start cleaning the window frame because Mr. Jensen would be out in a moment. In the meantime, he would have to excuse her, as she had things to do. When the door closed between them, the young man felt a surge of exultation as he opened his tool box. Mr. Jensen was about to get a surprise, his last, when he opened the door. The man's heart thumped against his ribs as he pointed the pistol at the door. Fifty thousand dollars just to pull a trigger. He'd leave the Embassy and travel around the world. Come on, Jensen! What's taking you so long? He would have pretty girls, one in every country, and live in only the best hotels. Come, please come! The wonderful food and sweets! He began to sweat a cold, uncomfortable sweat. Come, damn it! He looked about. He was alone. Ah, the doorknob turned. As it opened his finger pressed the trigger.

A calm voice said, "I'm Joe Jensen, Jim. You came here to kill me. Sorry, but not today. Hand me your gun and come with me. We have to have a talk."

Jim's finger turned white as he pressed harder and harder on the trigger. What could have happened? It always worked before when he practiced. Now his first real job and...

His hand felt numb as the gun was removed from him and his arm was held in a firm grip. For a moment he jerked to free himself, then gave in. A voice told him, "Sit here. My friends and I want you to tell us all about yourself. Take a few deep breaths and pull yourself together. Take your time, then start with your father and mother, sisters, brothers, schooling. Tell us of the pleasant things you remember most. Have no fear, understand? Good. Don't be confused, we intend you no harm. We want only to understand you, even to help you if possible. You want something to drink? How about a hot chocolate? Robert, will you please have Rose fix a large cup of chocolate for our guest?" Joe asked.

Jim's mind was racing. What's with these people, he thought? I was about to kill one of them, or all if need be, and they treat me like a guest. A new kind of fear touched him, one he couldn't understand. The chocolate, will it be poison? No. That Jensen could have broken my neck if he'd wanted to kill me.

"Come," Joe's voice urged, "where did you come from, your family?"

"My family," Jim began in a soft voice, barely audible, "my family lived in Baghdad when I was born. They called me Abu. My father was very political, a proud man, a terrorist who boasted of his training. I was to follow his ways. We moved about and really had no one place to call home for long. He taught me to use all kinds of weapons. When he returned from a commission, he would tell in detail how his group blew up an airport and killed so many Jews and Christians, or of how they had parked trucks or vans in front of Embassies or government offices to blow them up. I felt honored to hear that he had removed such unholy mortals who were destroying the earth, and I wanted to be like him."

Rose appeared with a cup of hot chocolate and handed it to Heather, who held it out to Abu. He took it without expression and held it for a time, warming his hands before sipping it. It tasted good and soothed his throat. In response he nodded and attempted a faint smile. They waited in silence for him to continue. When he had consumed half the chocolate, he seemed more relaxed and began talking as if to friends. They did not question or hurry him. He began to enjoy telling his story. No one had ever seemed interested before. This kind of treatment, this caring was something he was not prepared for. These people were not supposed to be like this. He was to give his life before giving up. His honor was to be attained in his next life. Not understanding politics, or even caring, he followed his father's teaching without question. What was difficult for him was living in the Embassy and seeing how people lived, worked, and played in this country. He was beginning to doubt his own father, who had lost his life just before Abu was sent here. The leaders said he was a hero because he took six Jews with him.

Palmer had sensed the doubts of the would-be terrorist and offered him a chance to escape. All he had to do was kill one man and then run away. Palmer would set it up and give Abu enough money to start a new life anywhere in the world.

The plans were set in motion after Palmer left. He paid one of the chauffeurs to drive Abu by the house to throw the rock and then take him to a garage later to pick up the glass truck. Abu looked up at each of them and said, "You know the rest. I think I am glad I failed. I don't think I'm very good at my work."

Joe smiled and asked Abu matter-of-factly, "What can you tell us about the five people in the house next door to the Embassy?"

"One of them was Palmer. Two are trained terrorists like me, but much older. And two are information gatherers. You call them spies. They spend a lot of time reading about art sales. Why, I don't know. I work in the Embassy itself as a clerk, checking passports mostly, and running errands. I have a small apartment about six blocks away."

Abu was now eager to tell all. He gave the address of the apartment and told how he was to receive an envelope with the money from Palmer from one of the two terrorists at the Embassy when he returned from killing Joe. The terrorists did not know what the envelope was for. They were only to give it to him when and if he asked for it. If he failed, he would be dead.

Joe glanced around at the others before speaking. "Abu, we're going to give you the opportunity to see the world, if indeed the money is in the envelope. You may return the truck after breaking the glass to give evidence that you were here. When you go back to the Embassy, collect the envelope, and leave holding the envelope in your left hand, after you're sure it contains the money. Then go and keep going.

"If the money's not there, walk down the street two blocks and turn left. We'll pick you up and decide whether to help you, and if so, how. If you decide to stay on at the Embassy, we'll understand, but one day we'll pick you up and you'll go to a Federal prison for many years. It's your choice."

Abu said nothing for some time. He looked at his captives before speaking. "Thank you. I am grateful and thank you for the opportunity."

He never did ask why or how they knew he was going to kill Joe. He left a happier young man than when he came. In response to one last question from Joe, he said that as far as he knew, the men at the Embassy had no plans to kill him. They were busy dealing with someone in the Pentagon about arms. This Heather promptly reported to Karp.

***

Robert returned to the breakfast table from the study. "It was the glass people on the phone. They wanted to know if someone would be here if they came to replace the window within the hour. You were saying that Abu received the money and is on his way, somewhere in the world."

"Yes," said Frank, "he waved good-bye to Darin and me, even though he couldn't see us. His smile was reward enough for our decision. I wish him luck and hope he doesn't come in contact with Palmer."

"Where do you think he'll go?" Heather asked.

"I hope he finds a small town and buys a cleaning business or something like that and becomes part of a community," Darin said.

"Joe," Heather said, "what do you think about the two of us going to Provence and taking a hot air balloon ride over the countryside? We might visit our friend, Palmer, and we could make it, in part, another honeymoon. I understand the light there is like no other place in the world. For a painter..."

"Hold on, H., you don't have to sell me. But another honeymoon? I haven't recovered from the last one! But, yes, it may be a good idea."

***

It didn't take Karp long to tie the Embassy man's connection to General Jerold Bluebill. It was agreed that Darin and Frank would visit the Pentagon together. The appearance of two men from their organization would carry a lot of weight. Even a general who wore three stars would hesitate to challenge the President's men.

Outside the general's office, however, the sergeant major said, "Sorry, General Bluebill can't be seen without an appointment, sir." The Sergeant major extended his erect posture another two inches and expanded his barrel chest, stretching polished buttons to the limit permitted by his neatly pressed uniform. His red face deepened as his eyes focused on Darin in a challenge of authority.

Darin said, "Just tell him we're from Karp. He'll understand."

"No, sir. I can't do that. You'll still have to make an appointment," the sergeant major insisted.

"OK, Sergeant Major, I'll make one right now." As Darin turned toward the office, the sergeant grabbed his arm. The next moment he crashed against the door and sat down against it. Darin turned the knob and walked in. Frank followed.

The general left his chair and shouted. "What the hell is going on here! Who the hell are you? Sergeant Major! Where are you?"

Darin held up his hand and the general fell silent, his face red with anger. Frank stepped aside so the general could see his man sitting on the floor. "Now, sir, we're from Karp, to talk about two gentlemen from the Iranian Embassy. Please dismiss the Sergeant Major and let's have a pow-wow."

The general's face turned a strange shade of green, but he returned to his desk and put on a brave front. Frank didn't wait for any questions or let the general compose himself. "We'll lay it on the line. We know all there is to know about your business with Iran, kickbacks and all. What you're going to do is tell your pals that a man named Palmer killed three of their terrorists two years ago and just recently informed some U. S. Government agents about the Iranians' tunnel to the second house. Repeat that to me—sir!"

The general repeated the message, then asked, "What about me?"

"After you pass along the message, you'll be permitted to resign for health reasons. I presume you do want to retain your health—ah, sir?"

"I believe I understand. Thank you, gentlemen."

As they left, the sergeant major gave them a murderous look. He received broad smiles in response. As they left the building, Frank said, "Guess that will cut off Palmer's home base."

***

Aix-in-Provence, in southern France, has an atmosphere of timeless peace with its old houses of warm stone, baroque fountains, and ancient churches. The countryside, with its pines and cypresses, aqueducts, and Cezanne's famous gray Mont Sainte-Victoire, was once controlled by Rome. Under brilliant light, it has played a transcending role in the responses of many great artists toward nature. Its dazzling light and intense blue skies continue today to seduce many painters, poets, writers, and lovers.

Cezanne was born here, and Picasso died not far away. Cezanne once said, "The great classical landscapes, our Provence, is where light is spiritualized."

Joe felt all this as he stood on the hotel balcony. His arm tightened around Heather's waist as he inhaled deeply. "I feel it ,too," she said. "It's marvelous, unreal. Maybe this is where you should paint. I could write, perhaps."

***

Some twenty miles west and a bit north from their hotel, just a mile out from the town of Borjols, stands a twelfth century monastery, now restored and privately owned by a Dr. J. C. Palmer. Dr. Palmer has yet to be seen by the locals. Just off the highway, a gate blocks the dirt and gravel road. Its rust encrusted hinges give evidence that it is seldom used. The rolling land, interrupted by acres of rocks, lies fallow. A double row of aged cypress trees screen the monastery. Just today word was passed in the town that smoke was seen rising from the chimney for the first time in recent years. The townspeople are looking forward to meeting their unknown neighbor.

***

"This morning we go for a balloon ride. I've set it up for nine o'clock just outside St. Maximim. That will put us about eight miles from Palmer's monastery as the crow flies," Joe said as he pulled on his gray coveralls.

Heather smiled as she zipped her coveralls. "Looks like a beautiful, clear, warm day with a light breeze. Perfect for an assault on a twelfth century monastery from the air."

Joe laughed, "That's one way of looking at it. That stack of ancient stones may have teeth if we find our man home."

"Do you think he'll be armed? It looks too beautifully peaceful for anyone to disturb with gunfire."

"Dear H., you are a poet. We're carrying dart guns."

"But they won't make noise."

"Well, let's pretend that Palmer is without fire power. Ready? Gear all together? Good. A kiss to start the day's adventure."

***

Their small rented car arrived at the field near St. Maximim, where three men were preparing the hot air balloon. A large fan was blowing at high speed, expanding the cavity that currently stood at about half its capacity. The wicker basket lay on its side. It would hold three passengers and four tanks of gas. One of the men welcomed them. "You are Monsieur and Madame Jensen, I believe?. I am Andre. I'm to be your pilot and shall try to take you over the area you requested."

"I'm Joe, and this is my wife, Heather. Looks like a good day for our flight." Joe extracted a small map from a flap pocket on his leg. "Do you know this monastery?"

"Oui, but of course, it's a landmark for us. Why?"

"We want to get as close to it as possible and perhaps land or just touch the ground long enough for us to jump from the basket. Then you can continue on your flight at a good altitude. Can you manage it?"

"Oui, if that's what you want. What about your return?" Andre asked.

"Continue past Barjols and land. After your chase van loads you, you can pick us up where the Monastery's road meets the main road. That should give you about an hour. If we're not there in five minutes, leave and we'll meet you back here."

Andre shook his head. "Well, as you wish, Monsieur. Have you done this before?"

The roar of the burners broke the morning quiet. Tongues of blue flame heated the captured air, and the balloon took shape as it rose above the basket.

"Let us go now," Andre shouted. The two men held the basket until the air-heated bag lifted. Ever so slowly it rose and drifted toward their destination. At 900 feet the burner fell silent. The air around them smelled fresh and sweet. There was no feeling of movement as they floated with the breeze. Only by looking down, seeing the earth drift by, could they judge their progress. Dogs barked without looking up, sensing their presence. Three ducks flew by and turned off when Heather waved. What a way to fly! The world could not be more beautiful—a true sense of peace, no conflict, a rare silence, as if dreaming.

"There it is," Andre said, pointing ahead. "How very strange, smoke is coming from its chimney. Someone is there."

"OK, Andre, let's drift over. When you pass the row of cypress trees try to set it down, just touching. Good. Release a little more air, now. Good. Ready, H.? Jump!" The burner roared as they left the basket, and the balloon seemed to shoot up and drift away. Joe and Heather lay flat against the earth until the balloon was well on its way. All was quiet. There was no response from the house. Looking through field glasses, Joe saw no sign of life other than a few field birds. No dogs, cats, chickens, horses, not even a car. The smoke changed color for a moment. Someone had just thrown more wood on the fire.

"Looks like he's unaware of us. Let's move in," Joe said. "Let's just walk to the trees as tourists."

In the trees they could hear music coming from the house, a popular French song. A flush of sparrows moved noisily about in the ivy surrounding an open window. They seemed disturbed by some movement from within. Joe signaled Heather to go around to the opposite side of the monastery and make her move. Everything remained still for several minutes. Only the music changed. Now it was rock, with a lot of high-pitched "oooo's." Then over the music came the sound of glass shattering. Heather had done her job. Joe took off and raced across the open area to the window, ignoring the close-by door. When he was within three feet of the window, he dived head-first through the casement, somersaulted, and came up on his feet. A figure had a 12-gauge shotgun aimed at the shattered window on the other side of the room. Joe's dart struck him in the back of the neck, and he wheeled around and fell to the floor.

The would-be killer laid supine on the stone floor. He appeared tall because of his extreme thinness. A dark blue turtleneck sweater extended his neck giving his bony cheeks and bulging eyes the appearance of a tortoise. A tight burr haircut enhanced the image. Moss green corduroy pants and worn tennis shoes completed the picture of a hungry young man desperate enough to even kill to enhance his position.

Joe called out, "It's OK, H. He seems to be alone." Heather's head appeared at the window. "Palmer?" she asked.

"No, unfortunately not. Looks like he hired a local or someone to look like one. See any evidence to suggest how he got here?"

"Yes, I found a bike. That must be it. Want me to come in?"

"Yes, we have to give this place a look," Joe said, bending over his victim. He tore open a small sealed plastic envelope and held it under the prostrate man's nose and pressed down on his chest. The body quivered, then relaxed again.

Heather arrived. "Anything I can do to help?"

"Check the rooms. I think he's alone, but let's be sure. I noticed a portable telephone. See if a number appears anywhere. I'll check his pockets."

"Who are you?" The drugged man's words were slurred.

"Never mind, it's more important for you to tell me what you're doing in my house," Joe said.

"Your house? But he told me it was his house. Who are you, Monsieur? I was paid to...mon dieu, never mind."

Joe removed the man's wallet and opened it. "You're Claude Fouch, yes? Your driver's license says so. Not too good a picture, but it's you. Why were you trying to kill me? Tell me or I'll change your sex here and now." Joe's voice convinced the man that talking was the easier way out.

"Oh well," Claude said, "I'll never see him again anyway. I was told this was his house and that a man—yes, you fit the description, monsieur—was coming here to kill him. He paid me ten thousand francs in advance, and I was to get another ten after—well, I was to call."

"You have the number? Give it to me," Joe demanded.

"No, I didn't write it down. I have it in my head."

"Well, tell me."

"It's 05-681. Yes, that's it. Now, tell me, how did you get here? I was watching the road. Nothing came near here, but a balloon, and it..."

"Never mind. Don't get up, just sit. Here's the phone. Dial the number and tell him it's done, and you want your money." Joe handed him the phone after pushing the numbers and waiting for a familiar voice to answer. "Bonjour," the voice said as Claude took the phone.

"Monsieur, it is done. No trouble. Now my money, if you please. Oui. Oui." The phone went dead. Joe took it and punched the numbers again, this time changing the last to a two instead of a one to identify the location of the number. On the third ring a voice said, "Marseilles Auto Repairs," and he knew. He hung up as Heather returned. "All's clear. About time we got to the road, Joe."

"Where are you to pick up your money, Claude?" Joe asked.

"It's here in the storeroom, off the kitchen, monsieur. Or so he said. What are you going to do with me?"

"Put you to sleep for the next four hours. You'll have no ill effects from your nap. But Claude, I advise you to find a different profession."

The dart pricked the side of his neck.

***

"Two minutes to spare. You made it just right," Andre said. They climbed into the chase van, and it returned them to their starting point. Thanks were exchanged, and Joe and Heather headed for Marseilles. Joe drove while Heather removed her coveralls and loosened her hair, then tied it into a ponytail.

"Perhaps we should stop at the airport on our way into Marseilles," Joe suggested. "I'll talk to security, and you visit the airlines. On a hunch, try Swiss Air. He may want to do some banking. He's been generous paying his hired hit men."

"Do you think he believes his man killed you at the monastery?"

"No, he knows he didn't. They had a key word or some other signal. Palmer plans too well to be easily fooled. He knew it would be dumb luck if he did succeed. He's playing with us, and we have to go along. We'll keep Frank and Darin informed and have them be our shadows. Sooner or later we'll need them and they'll be there."

They left highway A51 for A55 and soon turned off into the airport, where they found a parking area not far from the main terminal. Joe removed his coveralls, and after they secured the car, they headed, arm in arm, toward the busy terminal.

"Looks like everyone is on the go. Hope it will be possible to talk to some agents. It's a busy time," Heather said.

"All we can do is try. Maybe with luck, a few security men will get their attention. I'll leave you here and we'll meet in the cafe in half an hour." As Joe headed for the office, noticed a man eyeing him, trying to circle through the crowd to get behind him. The man was large, about two or three inches over six feet tall, and was wearing a blue beret and a plaid shirt. As he pushed toward Joe, he kept his eyes focused on him. Joe continued on his way until he got to a small area that was relatively clear of people. Easing his dart gun from inside his light jacket, Joe hesitated as if seeking directions, and turned slowly around just as the man started to thrust his arm forward. In his hand was a keen edged blade that reflected the overhead lights. His face registered amazement as the dart entered his neck and he began to fall. Joe half turned, like a dancer, and slipped the gun out of sight. Then he bent over the man and quickly removed the dart. "Someone get a doctor! This man fainted!" Joe called as he backed slowly through the gathering crowd.

He found the door marked "Securite`," entered, and asked a uniformed lady if he might speak to the person in charge. As he spoke, a porter entered and shouted for help. A man had passed out, he said, and might be dead. Two officers rushed out. A third officer appeared and was hurrying to catch up when the lady officer raised her hand and started to say, "Monsieur Roussell, Captain. This gentleman..." But the captain was not interested and started to push past them.

Joe grabbed his arm. "A moment, please. I know what the problem is out there. In part, that's why I'm here."

The captain came to an abrupt halt. "Monsieur, this had better be good, or you're in trouble."

"I'd like to introduce myself. May we go somewhere private?" Joe's demeanor reassured the captain, and he ushered Joe into the office and closed the door behind them.

"Now then, who are you, and what is the excitement outside?" the captain asked.

Joe unfolded a small sheet of paper that bore the seal of the Office of the President of the United States and handed it to the Captain. "This will introduce you to Joe Jensen who holds the highest position in my service. His identity should remain confidential.

Any service you may give him will be noted and appreciated. If verification is required call ———, signed, The President of the United States of America."

The captain sat down. "Well, well, Monsieur Jensen. I am impressed. Now, first tell me about the commotion, and then what I can do for you."

***

The maitre d' gave the Jensens a table by a window that overlooked a runway. After ordering lunch, Joe looked quizzically at Heather. "No, I had no luck," she said. "The agents were much too busy to give me any time, and the few I did talk to were of little help. How did you do?"

Joe recounted his activities and his meeting with the head of security, who at the moment had eight people checking on Palmer, or "Chapman." "He thinks the passport check may be the best bet. With luck, we'll know before we finish lunch."

As Joe was picking up the check, the captain appeared. He bowed to Heather, "Madame Jensen, Monsieur Jensen, your man left for Zurich a short while ago. Do you want me to have him held? A call will do it." He looked at his watch. "Barely. He may be on the ground, but we can try."

"Thank you, no, we will follow. Just keep the big fellow away from a phone for a couple of days. And you have our grateful thanks for your help." They shook hands as they parted.

"He's still trying. How close did the big man get to you?" Heather asked on the way to the car.

"I guess we spotted each other about the same time. He wanted to get behind me. That was his first mistake. Looks like Palmer isn't having very much luck in finding professional help, or perhaps..."

"You think he's hiring incompetent people on purpose?"

"Perhaps," Joe said.

***

They returned to Aix, and settled their bill at the hotel, then called Robert and asked him to have Frank and Darin meet them in Zurich. The rental car was left at the airport. As they boarded the plane, a small, dark-haired man pushed past Heather. She grabbed the rail with one hand and pressed the other on the man's back. She noted as they took their seats that he was sitting just two rows behind them. As Joe bent over, she whispered to him, then asked aloud, "Do you want the window or aisle seat?"

"The aisle is fine, you enjoy the window. The landscape is as beautiful as it gets anywhere." During the flight, the small, dark man walked the aisles twice, massaging strong, bony hands. Dark, dead eyes seemed unaware of his surroundings. He moved as if in a trance or on drugs. Deep red blotched skin stretched tightly over a bony face. He wore an expensive tailored Italian suite and highly polished shoes.

"How shall we play this?" Heather asked when the plane touched down.

"He'll make his try on the ramp as we debark, just before we enter the building. It'll happen fast. Stay behind him, and as he reaches behind his neck, break his arm. It will be most vulnerable in that position. Then walk past and let the confusion take over."

As the door opened, Joe took a bag in each hand. Heather let a passenger get between her and Joe. The small man pushed ahead of her and she followed. After leaving the plane, they continued down the jetway single file. When they were about six steps from entering the building, the man's right hand reached behind his head. Suddenly, he uttered a cry of pain and fell to his knees. His arm went limp as a stiletto dropped to the floor beside him. Heather stepped past the fallen figure, now lying on his side, supporting his arm with his other hand. Italian profanity flowed from his mouth as from a fountain. As Joe and Heather walked through the airport, Joe said, "Nicely done, H. That was one surprised assassin. Think there may be another before we get out of here?"

"I wouldn't doubt it. Someone could get killed if this keeps up. Want me to carry one of those bags so that you can have a free hand?"

"No, I'm all right. I'll depend on you to protect me, love." Joe held his arms out from his body, showing off his arm strength.

"Are you trying to impress me, Mr. Jensen?"

"Aren't you impressed? Well, OK, try harder."

They passed through the doors to the taxi stand and bus stop. The bus had two seats left, and they settled in as it took off. When they left the bus, they stopped in a shop for a sweet and coffee. Everything seemed normal. They hailed a taxi and gave the driver an address that would place them two blocks from a small hotel that the Special Services had used for many years. There they would meet with Frank and Darin in a day or two. The sub-basement of the Zurich hotel held an arsenal. It was considerably smaller than the facility Karp had in D.C., of course, but Joe could replace the darts he'd used, get electronic gear, if needed, and use a fax.

They walked the final two blocks to their hotel, checked in and went up to their room.

After bathing, Heather called Robert to ask if anyone had tried to approach the house and inquire about events. "What about your lady, Kathryn?" she asked him.

"Had dinner with her last night, Heather. She's still spending most of her time with her mother, who's not doing too well. Looks bad for her, and it's not helping my courting. Rose is fine, sends love to you and Joe. Frank and Darin are on their way with information from Karp. That's about it. Hello to Joe." They rang off.

Joe entered the room in his shorts, drying his hair with a bath towel. "What's the news?" he asked.

Heather related the conversation and added a question. "What do you think Karp is sending over with Frank and Darin?"

"Probably something on Palmer's hired killers, would be my guess. You have an idea?"

Heather only shook her head. "Wonder if our friend in the monastery woke up and left?"

"Let's find out," Joe said as he picked up the phone. He gave the operator a number from a card advertising balloon rides twice daily—See beautiful Provence from the air. By appointment only—"Hello, Andre. Joe Jensen. Fine, yes, no problem. Why do you ask?" Joe listened for some time then said, "No, I have no idea. I just wanted to thank you again for the ride. We'll be back one day. See you. Good-bye."

Joe turned to Heather, who was sitting on the edge of the bed. "Well, our friend Andre was on a flight with some tourist from Dallas, about a mile away from the monastery, when one end of the building blew up. From his description, it was a store room off the kitchen. They found the remains of a male. Unidentified. Looks like our would-be assassin got paid off in Palmer's usual manner."

"No honor among killers, I guess. Poor fellow never had a chance," Heather said.

Joe referred to a small notebook to find the phone number for the bank that held a numbered account for Palmer. He asked the operator to connect him and was told to stand by. When contact was made, he made an appointment with its president and secured its address.

***

In a small park opposite the bank Heather waited for Joe to return from his visit with its president. It was a pleasant wait on the sunny bench. The activities of pre-school children, snugly dressed to protect them from the chill, were closely attended by nannies, who wore lace-trimmed caps and long, flowing light blue capes. Small and large dogs barked at the spider monkey wearing green leather kinderholster and perched on the shoulder of the organ grinder with its arms around its master's head. A smartly uniformed officer bent over to caress the curls of a young nursemaid. It appeared a joyful world, without threat or unpleasantness. She started forming the words that one day would become a poem expressing the emotions of the moment.

"Ah! Daydreaming! It is a lovely little park. A few minutes of escape. What would the city do without its parks?" Joe bent and kissed her on the neck.

"Dear sir, you do set a young girl's heart aflutter," Heather said, giving Joe a most appealing look.

"You thinking of children?"

"Yes, but not in the way you may think. Tell me about the banker. Did he help you?"

Joe hesitated a moment, looking about. "Yes, after I identified myself. His computer showed a withdrawal yesterday just before closing, and it gave a local address. He was a little too eager that I notice it."

"Another set-up?" Heather asked.

"Most likely. Palmer has enough money to make this a good one."

"If he keeps this up, he'll run out soon. Killing isn't cheap these days." She looked about the park, sucked in a deep breath and sighed. What a strange world, she thought to herself. "Shall we walk back to the hotel?" She took Joe's arm and they walked through the park, enjoying its sights and sounds.

From a window in the bank a large man in a pin-striped suit watched them. Next to him was a smaller man, neatly dressed in a business suit and wearing a smirk. Palmer himself. The hairs on the nape of Joe's neck prickled as he hesitated a moment, then walked on. In a casual voice he said, "I feel him, Heather."

They returned to the sub-basement of the hotel, and Joe faxed Karp requesting a profile on the banker and the address he had been given. Back in the lobby he spotted a man and a woman on opposite sides of the room hidden behind newspapers. Joe chatted with the concierge a moment and learned that the two had been reading their papers for the past three hours. They had arrived five minutes apart and were unknown to the hotel. Joe walked up to the man and noticed his grip tighten on the paper "Pardon me, are you by any chance Rob Roberts?" Joe asked.

The paper lowered, exposing a hollow cheeked oval face that supported a Hitler-like mustache. Slick, red hair laid tight from a part that ran through the center of his freckled head. The reader's face flushed as their eyes met. "No, sorry, I can't help you." He returned to the paper, shutting off further conversation. Heather approached the other reader. "Pardon me, but aren't you Edina Perls?" she asked.

A voice behind the paper said, "No, I'm not."

"Are you, you sound as if you may be from Boston. I don't mean to disturb you, but..."

The voice said, "No! Now please go away. I'm waiting for my husband."

Heather reached for the top of the newspaper and lowered it. The woman met her eyes and angrily said, "Go away! I want to be alone!"

"Sorry," Heather said, "I thought you might be a friend playing a joke on me." The woman was quite upset and looked across the lobby to where the other reader sat. She was not unattractive other than her blue-green eye shadow and long lashes and bell-shaped felt hat resembled a Mata Hari.

As Joe and Heather entered the bar, Joe smiled and nodded to the concierge. They sat at a table where both readers would be visible and ordered tonic water with lemon, which they sipped as they nibbled from a bowl of small pretzels. "She was not very friendly," Heather said.

"He's nervous and wears a gun, shoulder holster. I imagine she's armed as well."

"If so, it most likely is a leg piece. Do you think we're their target?" Heather asked.

"Yes, but it's a guess as to where and when. They're not positioned very well to do it in the lobby. There could be more, of course, perhaps in the room or the elevator. Maybe we should get rid of the readers. What do you think?"

The waitress arrived with more tonic water, and Joe asked her if a phone was available.

"At the end of the bar, sir."

Joe returned in a few minutes and lifted his glass in a toast. "To love and high adventure."

Before long, the concierge approached the gentleman reader, exchanged a few words with him and escorted him to a waiting car. As the man bent over to speak to someone in the back seat, he was pushed into the car through the open door. It closed behind him and the car sped away. In a few minutes the second reader neatly folded her paper and went to the entrance, where she paused a moment before leaving the hotel. The concierge was standing at the curb as a limo drove up. She approached to ask him a question as he opened the car door, but before she could form her question, she was thrown in and the door closed behind her. The car pulled away into traffic.

"Two down and what to go?" Joe asked, lifting his glass.

"Your call set that up so quickly?"

"Yes, dear wife. Karp would be proud of his men here. They're checking the floors and our room for any surprises."

The houseman entered the bar, and Joe waved him over. "Find anything?" Joe asked him.

"I guess they have no idea just what we are here. We found three bugs. One was under the bed," he said smiling, "one was under the desk, and the third was in the valance over the window. Smart bastards, getting in. It couldn't have been our people. Anyway, the room is clear anytime you want to use it. We're holding the rooms next to and across from you for Darin and Frank. Karp's orders."

"Thank you. We may go up now and nap for a few minutes," Joe said. The houseman watched as they headed for the elevators and mumbled, in envy, "Have a good nap." His smile broadened, his thoughts would remain his.

***

The phone rang at seven and a familiar voice said, "We're here! Meet you in the basement in half an hour."

"What's that about, Joe?" the sleepy, contented Heather asked.

"They're here. Out of bed and get dressed. Plans are to be made my love, and news to be heard. We're due in the basement in half an hour. Come, we'll shower together."

"You know how to get a girl out of the sack," she said, throwing the covers off in a sweeping gesture, then pushing ahead of Joe as they entered the bathroom. "I'll adjust the water this time."

"Was it too cold before?" Joe asked slapping her bottom.

"Not cold enough. We have only half an hour."

***

The basement meeting room was small, but comfortable. It provided total security. The man in charge was Karp's counterpart and had worked with them in the past. He was known as Karl. There was a striking resemblance between the two men. Perhaps Karl supported a few more pounds and enjoyed tailored suits that he wore with pride.

As Joe and Heather left the lift, Karl met them. "Darin and Frank are waiting. Here are the faxes from Karp. Want me to join you?"

"Yes, Karl, please. Your help would be most welcome. You understand that this is personal in part and..."

"No need to explain. I know all about it. But it has grown into something much larger than a shoot-out between you and Palmer. Karp's fax will explain." Karl opened the door to the conference room, and they were greeted by Darin's booming voice and Frank's warm smile.

After a bit of teasing, they got down to the business at hand. "It's good to be together," Joe said. "Let me bring you up to date." He related the events since their arrival on the continent, a step behind the artful Palmer. Then he asked Karl about the two lobby readers.

"Well, they should soon be joining a tribe of Bedouins deep in the desert. No phone, no money. They'll have to work their way out, which should take at least a month or two. The lady was a tough one, carried a gun strapped to her thigh. He was a pussycat. They were both from the organization that Karp mentions in the fax. She gave us nothing. He was happy to tell everything he knew. It's coming together now."

"That's part of the information we have," Frank said. "Karp and company closed down a house in D.C. that was part of a world-wide organization of assassins for hire. Their calling card for the 'Heavenly Mortuary Co., Ltd.' shows an upside down butterfly on a tombstone. When one of them is commissioned to make a kill, he leaves the card with the person who hired him. To retrieve it, he must give proof of success. Failure means a fine of one-half their fee. If the money is right, they'll take on anyone. No one knows who heads the organization, but whoever it is has great wealth. We suspect that the people Palmer hired are members. The group seems highly organized, yet quite young, still recruiting, though how, we're not quite sure."

"They're young, that's for sure, if the people sent after H. and me are examples. However, I believe they were chosen purposely to lead us on, hoping that by some fluke, one of them would succeed. But then,

Palmer thinks I'm only a painter. Or does he? Well, regardless, it seems there's a tie-in between the bank president and the address given for Palmer. And my guess is that there's a connection between him and the Heavenly Mortuary Co." They all smiled when he said the name.

"Stranger yet," Karl said, "is that the number we have for their headquarters here is just across the street from where you think Palmer is."

"No, I don't think Palmer is or will be there. It's a set-up he feels I can't afford not to check. And he's right." Joe looked at Frank and Darin, who nodded. "We'll take our time and case both buildings, study their floor plans and perhaps close down another of their headquarters. Can it be set up that Frank and Darin can check the neighborhood buildings as city tax inspectors?"

"No trouble," Karl said, "uniforms and everything they need."

"Good. We must not be seen together at any time. Heather and I are hunting Palmer on our own, and whenever possible, you'll be our shadow, agree?"
Darin and Frank in unison said, "Agree."

"The fourth floor belongs to you while you're here," Karl said. "No one other than our staff, whom you know, should be there. If you're not sure, give this hand signal, and if they fail to respond in kind, well... Tomorrow night we should be ready to assault our target. We've had cameras set up for the last four days, and tomorrow we should have photos of everyone who entered and left the building."

Joe looked at Heather. "Karp would approve of this fellow."

***

As they left the dining room, holding hands, Joe suggested they take a walk before they returned to their room. Heather squeezed his hand in approval. It was a clear, starlit night with a refreshing hint of chill in the air. The city lights sparkled an invitation. They walked through the hotel door, held open by the uniformed doorman, and turned left up the slight grade of the sidewalk. Without warning, Joe was struck in the head by a heavy metal object thrown from behind the bushes. It was a glancing blow, but it dropped him first to his knees, then down on all fours. His eyes glazed and he passed out. Heather snatched up the object, which was rolling slowly down the paved walk, and was about to hurl it away when she saw that the pin had broken, rendering the grenade harmless. She handed it to the doorman. "Hold on to it," she commanded. "We'll need it later. Be sure the pin remains secure." She leaned over to check Joe's pulse, then rolled him over on his back. She kissed him as his eyes opened. Her face was the first thing he saw, blurred, but still beautiful. He smiled. "Now why did you do that to me?" he asked.

Two bellboys arrived and helped him to his feet. "Still want to walk?" Joe asked.

"Only to our room," she replied.

***

Leaning back in a cushiony chair, holding a cold compress against his temple, Joe asked, "Anyone see anything? Where it came from? Who threw it?"

"I caught only the barest glimpse. It was a slender man, maybe in his thirties, a plaid cap and a brown leather bomber jacket. He ran out of the bushes and across the street and disappeared between cars. I was focused on getting rid of the grenade. Don't understand how or why the pin left it harmless. Anyway, somebody up there likes you as much as I do."

"I don't understand these fellows. If they wanted to kill me with a grenade, you'd think they'd toss it like a baseball so that I'd catch it as a reflex. It should have been timed to explode as it reached me. The guy wasn't a soldier for sure. Whoever is recruiting for the

Heavenly Mortuary has little or no terrorist experience. He's most likely a business man—perhaps a banker—maybe even one we've met. Perhaps in the morning Karl's photos will let us know. Be a good wife and rub my head ever so lightly. The pain is fierce." A growing bump was approaching the size of half a golf ball with deepening colors of black and blue.

***

Little used railroad tracks ran behind the machine shop and assorted warehouses. A switch engine had uncoupled a box car, leaving it just opposite the shop. There was nothing strange about this event except that it happened just before dawn in an area at the edge of Zurich where older commercial buildings stood mostly unused and all but abandoned after working hours, except for an occasional watchman.

The machine shop stood barren, its equipment long removed. Only its oil-stained concrete floor, with protruding bolts here and there that had once secured lathes and drill presses, gave evidence of its past. A few dirty rags and metal filings clung in corners where sweepers had left them. The strange thing about this simple building was that it had double walls on each side with a two-foot walk-space between them. The reason for this had long been forgotten.

Just across the pot-holed street stood a three-story red stone building. Across its top was a decorative arch that held the carved date, "1876." A tarnished brass plate announced that it was the Ulrich Casket Co. In smaller letters beneath it were the words, in German, "Comfort for eternity." Three worn marble steps led to a double carved door that supported two thick, beveled glass windows coated with years of grime that the eye could not penetrate. A useless doorbell stood out from the wall like a breast, its bell button a red rubber nipple that continued to invite the finger. On either side were corrugated metal warehouses that stood empty.

The building was square and had a full basement. Each floor was divided into four rooms. A hallway and staircase ran through the center, with bathrooms at the far ends. The interior belied its outside, for it was clean and orderly. The third floor contained a kitchen and three bed-sitting room combinations. They were occupied. The parlor on the first floor contained five open coffins, exhibiting satin and tufted silk interiors that promised everlasting comfort. The walls were hung with sepia photographs of cemetery vaults and tombstones. A small desk set to one side held outdated pamphlets.

Light was admitted into the basement through six welled windows thirty inches below ground level, protected by steel bars. A camera's telephoto lens was focused on the front door from a water tower just beyond the tracks, back of the abandoned machine shop.

***

"Come on, now. Rise and shine. Its getting late, out with you Joe Jensen," Heather spoke as she pulled off the covers.

"Yes, yes, I'm with you. This kind of treatment wasn't in our marriage contract. Be gentle with your wounded spouse."

"Don't expect any pity from me. It'll get you nowhere. Now move."

Joe abruptly sat up, then eased himself back down again. "What a head I've got! That grenade really clobbered me. I guess it'll be tender for a few days. This bump feels like I may become a unicorn. How would you like that? But it's better than being blown to bits, I think. H. how about ordering breakfast sent up. It'll save time." He got up again and walked gingerly into the bathroom.

"Sounds good to me. Anything special?"

"Juice, oatmeal, toast, eggs, bacon, that sort of stuff, " Joe said as he lathered his face.

He was pulling on a turtleneck sweater when the waiter knocked. A voice said, "Breakfast."

Heather opened the door. "We're looking forward to it. Bring it in."

A thin faced man in his early thirties smiled at Heather. His tanned face appeared darker contrasting the starch white jacket. His eyes avoided contact as he wheeled the breakfast cart into their room.

Joe's head popped out from the sweater. "Have I seen you before?" he asked the waiter.

"Don't know sir. I haven't been here long."

Joe gave the subtle hand signal. He received no response in kind.

"If that's all," the waiter said, "I'll leave you."

"No, you won't leave. I want you to sit down and eat our breakfast. Let's start with the orange juice."

"I don't understand. Please, I must return to the kitchen. There are others to be served."

"Drink!" Joe commanded, as he signaled Heather to the phone.

The waiter tried to break for the door, but Joe grabbed his forearm and pressed. "Sit down! Drink half of each juice, then the coffee, and if you're still with us, we'll start on the rest."

The waiter paled, "I can't. No, no. It's poisoned, it'll kill me!"

Heather's eyes widened as she returned the phone to its cradle. "Damn!" she exclaimed.

"OK, tell us about it, everything." Joe smiled as the waiter collapsed in a chair. He suddenly seemed smaller but for his widening eyes that expressed fear. Heather nodded, indicating someone was on the way. "I was, they ah...were to pay me twenty-five thousand francs if, ah, ah, if I killed you. It was their idea. Perhaps because I was a professional waiter. How did you know? I..."

A knock interrupted them. Heather opened the door to two familiar faces. As she explained what happened, Joe asked the waiter where he had put the poison. "In the orange juice, only the juice. It's rare and difficult to obtain, a single drop should kill in a few seconds."

"Do you have any more, the vial?"

The waiter reached into his pocket and produced a glass vial smaller than the tip of his little finger. He handed it to Joe, who said, "You will go with these men and answer all their questions. They'll take the orange juice with them for you to drink if they think you're lying."

After they left, Heather remarked, "What a way to start the day."

***

Frank and Darin were in uniform as city officials consigned to inspecting the condition of the buildings in the block that contained the Ulrich Casket Co. and the abandoned machine shop. As they approached the marble steps of the casket company, its door opened and a smartly dressed woman appeared. She wore a black narrow-brimmed hat which supported a veil that hid her dark eyes in deep shadow. A tight, dark brown silk dress outlined a well proportioned figure. A wide black leather belt, held by a polished gold buckle, supported her erect posture. She was a lady of substance who was not to be disturbed by minor officials.

"Pardon me," Frank said, "we're city property inspectors. May we talk to you about this building?"

"No, no, I'm just visiting. Mr. Kroehler owns the building. I was just looking in on his sick wife. He is out of the country for the week. You'll have to return when he's here." Her soft firm voice was that of a cultured, well educated lady.

"We'll do that. We'll just walk around the building, make notes and leave. We won't disturb his wife. Thank you, and have a good day."

The woman gave a faint smile and descended the steps as a black sedan pulled up to at the curb. She entered, and it drove away.

"Now that's a pleasant looking lady," Frank said grinning. Darin nodded his head in agreement.

***

Joe and Heather were studying maps and floor plans when Karl arrived. They exchanged greetings, and Joe asked him about the poison. "You may be interested to know that a single drop of orange juice from your glass killed a lab rat instantly. Never saw anything like it."

Joe removed the tiny glass vial from his pocket and placed it on the table. "Perhaps you'd better have it analyzed and cut off the source, if possible. What about the waiter?"

"It's difficult to understand this outfit. They're not professional killers. They look more like a bunch of romantic misfits who were carried away by Robin

Hood stories. A pro like Palmer could only be using them to play his own game. As for the waiter, what he told us added little to what we already knew. He has no idea who the head man is. At the moment, he's also on his way to join the Bedouin tribe in the African desert." Karl laid a stack of 8 x 10 photos on the table. "Here are some of the players."

Heather and Joe moved closer to study the photos of the entrance to the building across from the machine shop. "Ah, this could be the one who threw the grenade. Let's set it aside," Heather said, removing the photo.

"Here's our man, Palmer himself. Set it aside, H. Here he is leaving. Note the date and time."

They went through the stack three times and separated out twelve photos. Three of the people were now in or on their way to Africa. Palmer appeared four times, coming and going. At the last date and time of his sighting, he was leaving the house. It appeared that five people were living there, one of them a woman. Other than Palmer, none were recognized as known criminals.

"It's reported that two of them stay in the machine shop on four-hour shifts and station themselves between the double walls—waiting for you, Joe," Karl said. "I suspect, from all we know of Palmer, that he won't be there. Most likely he's on his way elsewhere by now."

"What are your plans to close them down, Karl?" Heather asked. But before he could answer, Frank and Darin arrived to report their findings. Frank began. "The machine shop is set up to kill anyone who enters without authorization. The two men stationed between the walls have trapped themselves. They assume they're going to make their kill and walk away, poor bastards. There are six basement windows in wells. The glass is old and brittle. Six plastic packs with timers would bring the building neatly in on itself, if you want. Palmer most likely won't be there. It depends on how much you want to get rid of this outfit."

"Karl," Joe said, "I'll visit the banker again and let him know that early this evening, I'll visit the address he was so anxious for me to see. You cut off the telephone and power to the house to see who we can flush out. No use in destroying the house if we can squeeze the head man. The banker may be the local head. It would be better to have him think Palmer set him up. If he passes the word around, there may be more interest in getting rid of Palmer than in helping him.

"Palmer's pattern has been to leave clues along the way in case his paid assassins failed. I think he'll continue. This should be your party tonight, Karl. If you don't object, Frank and Darin will join you. Heather and I may move on quietly. We'll let you know where we land."

***

The receptionist told Joe that the president of the bank could give him five minutes only. As she opened the heavy door to his office, the banker called out,. "Mr. Jensen, what can I do for you? Did you find your man? What was his name—Palmer?"

Joe offered his hand and received the banker's soft, pudgy one in return. His expensive suit hung loosely over a huge flabby frame of gray flesh similar to the putty color of his puffy face. It was obvious that his exercise was at the table consuming rich foods in quantity. "No, haven't found him yet. Have you? Has he returned to the bank, by any chance?"

"If he has, I didn't see him. He could have done business with one of our officers. Shall I check?" The banker moved a filing card as if trying to hide it under a leather folder as he spoke.

"No, there's no need," Joe replied. "You could give me the address you have for him and I'll try it this evening. I've been called back, so this will be my only chance to contact him."

The banker pressed a button on his intercom.

"Yes sir," a soft, gentle voice responded.

"Marlene, please give Mr. Jensen the address for a J. C. Palmer. It's in the computer." The banker stood up, removed a handkerchief from a pocket, turned his back to Joe and blew his bulbous nose. "Excuse me," he mumbled.

Joe, as expected, took advantage of his invitation to read the card that protruded from beneath the leather folder.

"Now if you'll pardon me, I have another appointment. My secretary will give you what you want on your way out."

"I'm indebted to you for your help," Joe said, closing the door behind him.

Heather was enjoying the park again. The organ grinder was turning the crank on the cylinder, producing a lilting peasant tune. The spider monkey was doffing its felt hat to receive the pennies from the children. Lovers sat entwined on benches, whispering to each other. A balloon man stopped and offered Heather one to take home. A smartly uniformed soldier was flirting with her as Joe appeared.

"Sorry, soldier. You're too late. This lady is committed to me for the next hundred years."

In response, the soldier stood erect. "I salute you, sir. You have my congratulations. And I'm sorry I'm too late." He left them laughing.

"Now there's a man who'll win a lot of hearts," Heather said.

"Were you tempted?"

"I'll never tell."

"Before we walk back, look over my shoulder at the second floor window. Do you see a heavyset man watching us?"

"Yes."

"Is he alone?"

"Yes. Can we go? You know I was tempted to buy you a pink balloon with Mickey Mouse on it." Joe swatted her bottom.

"OK, let's go. I know a little chocolate shop between here and the hotel. If you behave yourself, I'll buy you the best cup of hot chocolate in all the world."

As they walked, Joe described his visit with the banker, adding, "That fellow was about as subtle as a meat ax. Let's hope he takes our bait and visits the Ulrich Casket Co. this evening. I'm convinced that Palmer is no longer here, but I'm looking for the time and place when he'll have to come to us. The word will spread fast, and he won't be able to hire help. His connections will refuse him, and then he'll be on his own. And that's something he's not used to. He's paid up front for this evening's attempt and will be waiting to hear the results in Paris."

"Do you think the banker is the top man in this so-called 'Heavenly Mortuary Company'?"

"No, my love. But, the important thing at the moment is that he's part of it. If he's the one who'll call Palmer to give him the news of our demise—and we get him at or near the machine shop—maybe he can be persuaded to tell Palmer we've been killed."

"I see. That might get him to relax his guard. Do you really think it could work?"

"Well, not really. But it's worth a try."

"Paris, that's a lot of city. Do you remember any background that would place him in a particular place or section of the city? Hotel? Cafe? Perhaps the Embassy?"

"Not the Embassy," Joe laughed. "He'll be persona non grata there. Unless you mean something other than the Iranian Embassy. We can check with Robert."

***

They stopped at the hotel's reception desk for the room key and Joe asked if they'd received any messages. There were none. "We'd best visit the basement," he said. They were admitted to the conference room by Karl, who seemed in an upbeat mood. "Good," Joe said. "I see that our comrades are here. I must send a fax to Robert, so please excuse me for a few minutes. H. will catch you up on my meeting with the banker." Joe closed the door and headed for the communications room.

A map and blueprints were spread about with various colored lines drawn to indicate strategies for the evening's assault. "I see you have this all worked out," Heather said. "Looks good. When do you pull the phone?"

"We're on the line. As soon as the banker calls, we'll cut him, and when he shows, the power will go," Karl said. "How sure are you that he'll come?"

"It's our best guess. Joe's idea is that Palmer is in or on his way to Paris and will be waiting for a call to learn the results. It's a long shot, but Joe has an instinct about these things. He feels that if we scare the banker enough, he'll call, or maybe we can stage our deaths, make him believe his men were successful. That would relax Palmer and then maybe he'd come out into the open."

"That may compromise things a bit as they now stand. Let's see what Joe thinks after reviewing what we have."

After Joe reviewed the plans, he said he saw little problem in working within them. He made his suggestions, and after about an hour they were in agreement. As they were leaving, Joe was handed a fax from Robert.

Karl said, "We leave in one hour, five minutes apart, in two nondescript cars."

***

Darin asked what the news was on the home front as Joe read the fax.

"All's quiet. I asked Robert to check anything that connects Paris and Palmer. He came up with three: a favorite hotel, The Maurice; a house in the Sarcelles area, not far from the Aeroport Le Bourget; and an address in Montmarte. They're far enough apart that if we get a phone number, it could help locate him. Oh, and Robert does mention, and I quote, 'Romance back on track'."

"Sounds serious. Who's the lady? Have we met her?" Frank asked.

"I know nothing about her except that brother Robert says she is the most of everything and all that any man could want."

"Now be careful, Joe, you may be putting your foot in your mouth."

"I know, love, just a fact of life."

Darin broke in, "Do you want us to follow you to Paris?"

"Yes, as soon as possible. H. and I will try to get rooms at the Maurice and with luck, we might find ourselves alone in an elevator with Palmer. What odds would you give on that?"

"Shall we remain in the shadows?" Frank asked.

"Yes, until we have him, don't be far away. You know the routine. Now, are you ready for the showdown at the Ulrich Casket Co.?"

***

It was on the far side of twilight when Joe and Heather drove slowly past the machine shop and stopped next to the broken curb. The street was deserted. A distant street light flickered feebly. Only the warm glow from the third floor windows of the

Ulrich Casket Co. gave any sign of human life. A large brown rat, its back hunched high, was fleeing across the street, pursued by a second one.

Behind the glass of the parlor window where the coffins that offered eternal comfort lay on display, the lace curtains moved a bit. The watery eyes of the banker waited to witness the killing that would earn the organization its fee. He watched as Joe and Heather opened the metal door and entered the darkness of the shop—then flashes of light and the sharp report of gunfire. A figure staggered through the door and fell in the street. A vast amount of blood flowed about the body. The banker disappeared from the window as silence fell. Outside, the rats were indifferent to the noise as one mounted the other in the shadow of the curb in hopes of increasing their population.

***

The banker had just completed his call to Paris when the front door sprang open, the lock broken by Darin's weight. He stepped in quickly, followed by Frank and Karl. They made surprisingly little noise, and the banker caught sight of them only as he was returning the phone to its cradle. With wide eyes, he screamed.

"Who the hell are you? What do you want?" he asked.

"We want a fitting for a coffin. Your size will do." Darin's deep voice frightened him. "And we're not from the 'Heavenly Mortuary Co.'"

That shook the banker, who stammered. "What do you...what's the Heavenly Mortuary...?" he asked in a hoarse whisper.

"Come now, Palmer told us all about it. He also said that you were going to kill a couple, and we see you did it—an American painter and his wife, who were looking for Palmer," Darin said angrily. "Now there's going to be hell to pay. You should have known you were being used and double-crossed. That's Palmer's way. So think, fast. You're in quicksand up to your chin and sinking fast. Who and where is the head of the Heavenly Mortuary. Tell us or..."

The blood drained from the banker's face turning his putty colored face ashen white. "I'll tell you what I can if you..."

"No deals. You're lucky we don't skin you and hang you up to dry."

In a small, dead voice the banker began. "I am head of Alpine unit number six of ten worldwide..."

***

Across the street Joe got up and brushed off the blood-colored sand he had poured from the plastic bag he carried. Heather stood by. "That was quite a performance. You're a ham for sure."

Frank joined them, grinning. "We got him. He's telling everything. The call went through to Palmer. At the moment he thinks you're dead, but that can last only a few days unless we plant a story that an unknown American couple...that sort of thing."

"Worth a try," Joe said. "But now I want to thank Karl's men for taking the gunmen out and setting things up so well. Then we'll get ourselves ready to fly to Paris."

"What is Karl planning for these people? Are they all going to end up in the desert with various tribes?" Heather asked.

"Yes, something like that. It's cheaper and more expedient than the court routine, which could take years. They know they're protected as they pull the trigger, and they demand their rights when they're caught. With Karl's system, it's quite a shock when they wake up to find themselves on a bed of sand with nothing but the clothes on their backs. Can you imagine opening your eyes in the middle of nowhere and seeing a dark figure against a cloudless sky standing over you? It's pretty scary to see someone like that who doesn't speak your language and isn't interested in your protest, or claims to your rights," Joe said thoughtfully. "It's one way to solve a lot of problems."

"Well, let's give this place back to the silence of the night."

Joe smiled and said to himself, "It's a night for the rats."

***

Paris, Paris, Paris. A city the world loves, a city people dream of. Paris is endless verse that expresses the joy and love for all things. It wears a patina burnished with love and caring. Every moment is a visual delight to capture the mind and soul of the artist. Its beauty entices lovers to give of themselves.

"Wake up, H., daydreaming? We're about to land. Look out and you'll see the Tour Eiffel. See it—there!" "Joe, kiss me—Wait a minute, do you know what color the tower is?"

"Of course, it's, it's—everyone knows it's, ah, gray."

"No it's not. It's strange, but very few people really know. They take it for granted."

"Well, what color is it?"

"Would you believe it's pumpkin colored?"

"Pumpkin! How about that."

"We should be on the ground in a few minutes, at Bourget," Joe told her. "We'll rent a car and check the house in the Sarcelles area. It's just north of the airport."

As they passed into the shelter of the terminal, a slow drizzle started, the kind that promised days of grayness. It was a few minutes after one when they approached the car rental desk, but the bright lights of the terminal contrasting with the deep gray sky made it feel much later.

"You notice anything?" Heather asked. "No one has attempted to kill us in the past few minutes. You think he believes we really are dead?"

"Could be. But we won't assume anything. What do you know of this area? Ever been in these parts before, H.?"

"No, I have no idea about it We'd better explore it. Flying in, it appeared to be a mixture of open fields, commercial warehouses, and a scattering of old, farm-like houses, then a grouping of apartment buildings.

***

"Your car will be available just outside Mousier in a few minutes," the rental agent said. "Take 114 right as you leave, then turn right again on 112, and that should take you to your address."

Joe thanked him. They started to leave when Joe said, "Another moment. Have you seen this man?" He held out a photo of Palmer.

"Oui, I have. He rented a car like yours. One moment. Ah, here it is. James Chapman. Is that right Monsieur?"

"Yes, that's right. May I note his license number?" Joe smiled, "Any hint of where he was going? We'd like to surprise him. Haven't seen him for some time." The agent shook his head as he wrote the number on a small pad and handed it to Joe. He wished them luck and turned to a waiting customer.

***

The car turned onto a deserted road with ancient chestnut trees, where a solitary farmhouse stood. What used to be a barn was now a foundation piled with rubble. Next to it was a broken tractor, about 1917 vintage, which gave no hint of what color it might have been. A stone milk house was the lone serviceable outbuilding.

The three-story house stood proudly, defying the ravages of age. Its cement color, wetted by the persistent drizzle, seemed to glow. Heavy shutters protected the windows. They had been painted recently. No light escaped from its windows, no smoke from its chimney.

"This must be the place," Joe said. "It's rather beautiful. What a history it must have! I can envision what it looked like before the first great war, perhaps even when Napoleon was Emperor. Shall we walk around it?"

He didn't wait for her reply, but pulled off the road between a couple of chestnut trees and stopped the engine. They sat in silence as the drizzle clouded the windshield. Heather opened the door, and Joe followed. Suddenly, the silence was broken by the roar of jet engines. The plane went directly over the house, climbing through its take-off altitudes, and they could feel the ground vibrate.

"Well, that explains why it's no longer a place for constant living," Heather said. "How many times a day do you think that happens?"

"Who knows. Anyway, no one has been here recently. No signs of recent entry. Let's go in and have a look." Joe used a piece of plastic from his pocket to unlock the door. When he pushed it open, they were met by a rush of stale, musty odor. Joe tried a light switch, to no avail. When their eyes adjusted to the darkness, they found a kerosene lamp on a side table and a small, antique compote that contained matches. Joe removed the lamp chimney and turned the wick up and down to distribute the kerosene before he lit it and adjusted the flame. With the light from the lamp they saw that the house held antique furniture that was covered with dust sheets. They were surprised to find a beautiful Italian landscape by Corot hanging in the parlor. None of the other paintings came up to the Corot. It was out of place in such company. A locked closet under the staircase concealed a small arsenal.

"Shall we disarm it?" Heather asked.

They spent the next hour pulling fuses and disabling firing pins. Careful to leave no trace of their presence, they locked the door behind them and returned to the car. They stood in the misty glow looking at the house as another jet passed overhead. Quickly they jumped into the car and closed the doors hoping to escape some of the earth-shaking roar.

***

At the desk of the Maurice Hotel, Joe filled out the registration card as Heather wandered about the lobby, which echoed with memories of many great personages who had been guests there. Among them was the general who was in command of the German troops in Paris during World War II. Having mined with enormous quantities of high explosive the sewers and bridges to destroy the city as the Germans withdrew, he refused, in the end, to give the order. He avoided Hitler's calls, wanting to know, "Is Paris burning?" The footsteps of Nazi boots in the hallways have long been replaced by genteel conversations fitting for the formal decor.

"Can you tell me," Joe asked the desk clerk, "has a Mr. James Chapman registered?"

"Just a moment, Monsieur, I'll check."

Heather placed her hand on Joe's shoulder and whispered, "This place is like being in a time warp. I feel the presence of the past. What stories it could tell!"

"Here we are. I am sorry, but Monsieur James Chapman checked out a few hours ago, leaving no forwarding address. How long will you and Madame be with us?"

"We can't tell. Sorry," Joe said.

"No problem, I see that you are privileged to come and go, and space will be available. We are accustomed to such arrangements." He snapped his fingers, and a smartly uniformed bell boy appeared.

***

Joe stood at the balcony window looking over the Jeu de Paume that housed the pictures of the impressionists to the Tuilleries gardens at the Louvre, revisiting favorite paintings in his mind. The drizzle distorted the glass, giving the view the appearance of a Seurat drawing. The city's lights were surrounded by multicolored halos. The sound of Heather's voice singing a French nursery tune drifted sweetly from the bathroom. She appeared, wearing a large white towel. "Such a lovely song! Where did you learn it?"

"I don't know what brought it to mind. Perhaps the warm comfort, feeling secure. My mother sang it to me on special occasions so very long ago."

Joe started toward her when the phone rang. "You're saved by the bell," he said, picking up the phone. "Who wanted to be saved?" she said, dropping the towel and turning her back to him.

"Been waiting for your call. Are you settled? No, we just missed him by a few hours. Heather? Well, at the moment I think she's feeling frustrated," Joe turned and winked at her.

She picked up the towel and threw it at him.

Joe ducked. "I suggest you stake out the farm house," he said into the phone. It won't be overly comfortable because of the jets taking off, but ear plugs may help. Tell Darin to take plenty of food and a large thermos of coffee." Joe explained in detail what they had found, including the arsenal under the stairs. He answered a few questions and then told Frank that after a good dinner, they'd check out the address in Montmarte. As he hung up, he turned his attention to his beautiful wife. She was fully dressed for the evening. "You know, Joe, I'll bet Robert wouldn't treat his Kathryn like..." His kiss silenced her.

***

Now and then a lone figure appeared, then disappeared along the narrow streets. A light fog held the lights captive. The raw female voice from the open door of a cafe was abruptly shut off as the door closed. A small silver stream of water ran against the curb, dancing like an endless ribbon. Bursts of laughter punctuated the mist. This was where Modigliani, Sutine, Pascin, and Utrillo once lived. Before them came Renoir, and later Picasso, and Braque. These streets had known misery, as well as the joy of good companionship. And now, under the cover of heavy skies and a shrouding mist, two hunters were stalking a deadly prey.

House numbers were hard to identify in the poor light and peeling paint.

"This should be it," Joe illuminated a small sign, "Atelier Anton Civet," with a pencil flashlight. It was a narrow door that opened onto a steep stairway, barely wide enough for two. It was squeezed between two galleries whose walls were hung with schlock paintings, souvenirs for eager tourists.

"Shall we go up?" Heather asked.

"No, I think not. It feels deserted, but it would be a bad place to be trapped. Let's return tomorrow as tourists and hope we'll have better visibility. It would help if this drizzle would blow out."

"Sounds good. Let's go back to the hotel and start over where we were before Frank called."

They walked across the street and looked back at the building. It had three large studio windows and three small windows covered by painted wood shutters that held many coats. Heather shivered and turned to Joe. "I know, I feel it," he said.

Unseen eyes watched them from one of the small windows as they disappeared into the mist.

***

The oncoming lights penetrated no more than five feet in front of the bumper. The car looked like a distorted, hazy white ball with pinpoint eyes,

"We must be almost there. You see any chestnut trees?" Darin asked Frank, who was leaning his head out the window to better see as the heavy mist varnished his face. The lights of the nearby airport glowed through the fog and silhouetted the farmhouse.

"I think I see it. It looks like a Charles Adams setting. Where are we going to hide the car? How about pulling off between the last two chestnut trees," Frank said.

"Why don't you get out and guide me. No use getting stuck."

Frank stepped out and tested the ground between the trees before motioning Darin to pull off and cut the lights and engine. They leaned against the car in the stillness and wondered what the hell they could do besides wait. They should camouflage the car with branches and leaves, but to walk a dozen feet away in the fog would chance being lost.

"Any ideas?" Darin asked.

"Yes, let's have a cup of coffee."

"Good. You pour."

***

Joe left the bed and hurried to the window to be certain that what he saw was true. Yes, there was the sky at last. It was blue and at the moment was being etched by the growing white line of a vapor trail. He was fascinated by the tiny dot creating the straight white line that held so firm.

"H., wake up, come see! Paris is waking up to a rare blue sky. Come on, we'll pretend we're tourists today, so let's have a tourist breakfast and visit Montmarte. We'll wear our cameras, dark glasses, and brimmed hats. And we'll buy a genuine painting of a fake street scene after Utrillo."

Heather sat up rubbing her eyes. "What are you saying? You want to buy a painting? A genuine fake? If you do, I want to pick it out. I know a pompous museum director we could present it to."

"Well, why not. I have a dealer friend who did that. He gave a pirate ship painted on black velvet to the local museum of director as a Christmas gift. But the fellow failed to see the humor. They have very delicate egos, for the most part."

"Well, now that you have me awake, let's get with it. But first, let me share the rare blue sky with you." The vapor trail still held its line some forty thousand feet above the famous palace where now hung masterworks of great taste.

The thought of the thousands of tourists who visited the great collections that Paris offered and then bought junk paintings as souvenirs to adorn their living rooms made Joe shiver.

***

They found the city as all visitors want to remember it. It was as alive as an ant hill just disturbed by a stick. The Parisians who were not scurrying to work were out walking about to welcome the bright sky. The murmur of city noise promised to develop into a din by noon. After the long, gloomy drizzle, it was a celebration welcomed by all—except those who were hunted.

Palmer's bony frame stirred on the lumpy mattress that lay on the old coiled springs. The small amount of light that penetrated from between the louvers gave only a hint of the brightness of the morning. He would have to find a public bath and steam, then a massage to get rid of the discomfort from the offending bed. He wondered about the two figures by the door last night. Was it possible that Jensen and his lady had not been killed as reported? The banker said he saw Jensen fall, bleeding heavily. He would ask the local office of the Heavenly Mortuary Company to find out for him. He was sick of this. He wanted to return to the Maurice and move about freely, find a woman and try to make up for the two years lost in that damned basement.

He went to the studio and stood before the skylight. What a day! He hurried to dress and escape his dreary surroundings, knowing that this had to be a good day for him. But then, all the city felt that.

The masseur had good hands, and the bath and steam did wonders for him. After a late breakfast, Palmer hailed a taxi and gave the address of the Chevillier Funeral Parlor. He was greeted by a tall, slender, middle-aged man in a pin-striped morning suit with balding hair that revealed a red freckled scalp, who inquired in a drawl if he could be of service. Palmer gave his name and asked for the director. The man invited him to be seated, then left him. It was a long wait. The atmosphere that was intended to give comfort and silence for reflection made him strangely nervous. He fidgeted while examining his bony hands. How could that damn painter have escaped his traps? Granted, the men he'd hired were not seasoned killers, but surely the odds would run out. He'd left clues to where he would be, and they were picked up. Well, he would kill the painter himself if he had to. Hadn't he waited at the top of the staircase most of the night on the chance his instincts were right about Jensen? His thoughts were interrupted by the voice of the pin-striped man, who said that the director would see him now.

"Follow me," Palmer was ushered into a large velour walled office that deadened the sound of the voice.

"Well, well, so you're the infamous Mr. Palmer. I've been getting a background on you as you waited. We're tempted to kill you and cremate you right now. You're not welcome here. You're responsible for the demise of our Alpine operation and the disappearance of several of our men. You used us and misused us. Now I suppose you want more help. Well, you're not going to get it from us. Who is this Jensen anyway?

"I saw a notice in the Zurich paper that a couple named Joe and Heather Jensen are supposed to be dead, but our people could find no proof of it. It's rumored that you killed a Senator Jensen, and that this fellow we were to kill is his son. If that's true, I hope he isn't dead and he's after you. Now get the hell out of here and never seek another contract with us!"

Palmer remained silent. The size and weight of the nameless director as well as the fire in his eyes suggested retreat. Retreat he did.

***

"Oh God! What a night!" Darin said, stretching his huge frame.

"Yes, and what a beautiful morning. We'd better get set for a long stay. Let's look this place over." Frank's words were lost in the roar of the first of several jets. "Joe was right about the ear plugs."

They split up to cover the grounds around the house. A small water tank, surrounded by a three-foot high mound, stood about a hundred yards from the house. An unused road ran on its far side. They drove the car to that road and covered its roof with branches and leaves. A telescope brought the house into sharp focus. They swept away all signs of their auto tracks, then entered the house and explored it thoroughly before returning to the car for a long wait. There was no escape from the roar of the great jets. They threw stones at them to preserve their humor.

***

As Joe and Heather entered the gallery, they were greeted by a short, eager little man who might have come from a Lautrec painting. He was rubbing his small fat hands together and exposing bad teeth giving a broad smile of welcome. His tight skin glistened with after shave that failed to evaporate. "Oui, oui, Monsieur and Madame. You are interested in a picture to invest? We guarantee the paintings are by the best of French artists. We deal only in genuine hand-painted pictures. What subjects might you prefer? Montmarte scenes are most valued. One hundred to five thousand francs. That includes the frame, of course."

Joe held up his hand to stop his spiel. "I am a painter and I..."

The dealer broke in. "I have too many painters now. The gallery couldn't afford to take on any more."

"That's all right," Joe said. "I wanted to inquire about the studios above you."

"Oh, I understand. You want to rent a studio? They are famous, you know. Many great painters started their careers there. Two are available on the top floors. No one is in the first, but it is rented."

"Good, may I look at them now?"

"They are expensive. Twelve hundred a month."

"Let me see them."

"Oui, I'll get the keys from the drawer and turn the power on."

"You control the power from here?"

"Yes, of course, in case the rent is not paid."

"Who would be my neighbor if I decide to move in?" Joe asked.

"Don't worry, the man travels the world and has paid for three years in advance. He is seldom in. It has been two years or more. Here are the keys for the two upper studios. Be sure to lock everything when you're finished."

They unlocked the street door. The steep hall stairway was illuminated by neon tubes that eliminated all shadows. The switch was activated by the opening of the door. Tracks in the dust-covered steps showed that a visitor had recently come and gone. The footprints disappeared at the door on the first floor landing. Joe inserted a plastic card to open the flimsy door, and Heather switched on the single ceiling light. There was a faint odor of recent occupancy. The bed held a slight warmth. Joe removed a pair of black socks from the floor beside the bed. "Our man was here last night. We missed him by an hour at most."

Heather said, "By the looks of the sink, he left without washing. His toothbrush and paste are unopened." She turned on the faucet and a dark brown, brackish stream of water coughed its way out. "Well, artists are supposed to suffer. Joe, did you suffer?"

"Never had the privilege, I'm afraid." He stood by the shuttered window looking at the street. "Bet he was watching us. He'll go somewhere to bathe and then visit the local Heavenly Mortuary Co. at the Chevillier Funeral Parlor to check on us."

"Think he'll return here?"

"No, I think he'll get nowhere trying to get help anytime soon. His source of hired assassins has dried up unless he can find some other lead in the underworld. That would take time. His best shot would be to set up something at the farm house."

"Why doesn't he set it aside for a year or so and then just walk up behind us on a crowded street, and—powie?" Heather asked.

"He can't think that way. He committed himself by having the rock thrown through the window. He has no scam going, and he's burned a lot of bridges behind him. Besides, he's obsessed by revenge. His ego just won't let him reason. What other game is there?"

"I'm sure you're right. Shall we tell the dealer you feel the need to suffer, but not in these pleasant surroundings? Shall we buy one of his hand-painted..." After returning the keys and using the telephone book for the address of the Chevillier Funeral Parlor, they thanked the dealer who called after them from the door, "How about 800 francs? You won't find a better studio in the city, left or right bank."

***

The taxi pulled in under the porte cochere and discharged its passengers. Joe asked the driver to wait. "We shouldn't be long. If we're not out in fifteen minutes, come in. We may need an excuse to leave."

As they entered the funeral parlor, Heather gave her most disarming smile to the slender man who greeted them. "Are you in charge, Monsieur?" she asked as he approached. He returned her smile and asked, "May I be of service? Our director is occupied at the moment."

Joe said, "We want to speak to your director about making arrangements for a person named Palmer. Will you be kind enough to tell him?"

"And who may I say wishes to speak to him?"

"Mr. and Mrs. Joe Jensen."

"I'll see if he can oblige you. Please be seated."

When the man disappeared, closing the door behind him, Joe walked slowly about the room, stopping before the chair where Heather sat. He leaned over to kiss her and whispered, "We're on camera-voice record." Then aloud he said, "Think they may know we're not alone?"

"If they've heard about the Alpine, they should be glad to get rid of Palmer. Besides..." Heather was interrupted by the return of the man who had greeted them.

"This way, please. The director will be most pleased to see you." His deep, drawling voice did not change, nor did his expression. They were shown into a large office. Its walls were a deep red velour, lavishly decorated with burnished, gold leaf rococo-framed pre-Raphaellite paintings that glowed from picture lights hung above them. On a deep pile Chinese rug stood a large rosewood desk ornamented with polished brass eagles. Behind it sat a huge man wearing large, horn-rimmed glasses that magnified his eyes.

"You, sir, may not know how much I wanted to meet you. Just what are you besides professing to be a painter? And what do you want from me?"

Heather moved away as if looking at one of the paintings. "Please Madame, stay with your husband." She ignored him as Joe spoke.

"You have nothing to fear from us. As you know, I want Palmer, and he wants me. He is no longer an asset to you, and if you still feel obligated to do us harm, I assure you, you'll have the wrath of God fall on you. Now tell me, has Palmer been here?"

"I understand that your threats are realistic. It was not my decision to do business with Palmer. Yes, he was here. He left about an hour ago. If I could tell you where he went, I would. Now, if you will be kind enough to leave, I propose to disappear."

"H., let's go and let this gentleman disappear before his unwelcome guests arrive."

As they returned to the waiting taxi, Heather said, "Looks like the ball may be in Darin and Frank's court. Shall we join them?"

***

They returned to the Maurice so that Joe could call Robert. The line was busy, so he called Karp. A sleepy voice said, "Joe, I've been waiting to hear from you. Are you both all right?"

"Has the local office been keeping you informed of the Heavenly Mortuary group?" Joe asked.

"We've been on top of it. I'm holding the last fax that said you and Heather were seen entering the Heavenly Mortuary offices and leaving about fifteen minutes later. Want to tell me about your visit?" Joe gave Karp a detailed report and then asked about any other connections that Palmer might use.

"Joe, try to catch him in the Paris area if possible and end it. There are two possibilities, perhaps more, but we suspect only two. Palmer has some connection with a barge in the Zaandam-Amsterdam area and a bookstore in Cologne. We'll cover them just in case. Do you know where he is at the moment?"

"Our guess is that he's heading for a farm house outside the city. Frank and Darin are covering it. We'll join them before long. I'll call you again and let you know if anything happens."

A few minutes after his talk with Karp, the phone rang. "Your Washington call is ringing, Monsieur Jensen," the operator said.

"Hello—Jensen residence."

"Rose, this is Joe. How are you? We miss your cooking. We're in Paris. Yes, today the sun is warm and the skies are blue. Is Robert there?"

"No, Joe, he went to pick up his lady, Kathryn, and they plan to take the boat and sail all day."

"Sounds very pleasant. Wish Heather and I could be with them. Well, leave word. We hope to be back soon."

"How are things on the home front?" Heather asked.

"Rose said everything is quiet. Robert is taking the boat out on the bay with Kathryn. Looks like their romance is blooming. As for Karp, he suggests we'd better reach Palmer before he leaves Paris. Let's go visit Frank and Darin."

"We should take some fresh bread and cheese, perhaps a couple of good bottles of wine."

"And some sweets for the big man," Joe added.

"What about firepower?"

"We have enough."

***

An enormous jet thundered by directly overhead as their rented car turned onto the road to the farm house. About a hundred yards ahead a panel van moved along leisurely. Joe slowed to match the van's speed and watched it turn into the yard by the house. As they came abreast of the van, two men in black work clothes stepped out and walked to the door. Another plane roared over. The men stopped and covered their ears, paying no attention to the other car, which had stopped nearby. When the jet was far enough away, one of the men inserted a key and opened the door to the house. They disappeared within, leaving the door open.

"Let's go," Joe said. As he and Heather passed the chestnut trees, they saw Frank and Darin running toward them. Joe motioned them to take the van while he and Heather headed for the open door. They entered quietly and stood just outside the parlor.

"This is it as described to us. Rather beautiful, don't you think? Corots bring a good price, especially the Italian landscapes that have buildings."

"Yes, I know," said the second man. "Let's get it wrapped and out of here before another damn jet comes over."

Joe said, "We've been had!" He rushed outside and looked about just as a bullet exploded in the wall behind him. "Down H.," he yelled as he hurled himself to the ground. The second bullet would have passed through him. Joe noted its direction as he ran for the shelter of a chestnut tree. Two more shots struck the tree. He peered around the tree to see a figure climbing down from a platform on the back of a pickup truck. "Check out the pickup!" he yelled to Frank and Darin as he ran to the van. He was sure the shooter would be long gone by the time they could get inside the airport. "Take our car and go. We'll take care of things here."

When Joe returned to the house, Heather was talking to the two men, who looked frightened and bewildered.

"These gentlemen are employed by the Drouot Auction House, Joe. They were ordered to pick up the Corot and deliver it to their warehouse. This envelope was to be left on the mantel. They presume it's a receipt." She handed the unopened envelope to Joe. "Bet I know what's in it."

"No bet, H., let's see." He took it to the front door and held it to the light. He wanted no further surprises. The envelope was addressed to Monsieur James Chapman.

"You gentlemen go ahead and deliver the painting. It looks as if everything is in order. We'll stop by the Drouot later today, or perhaps tomorrow."

They watched by the door as the van moved away with its precious cargo.

"No longer, Joe, open it. I want to know what he wrote."

"Now, now my lovely bride, be patient. Let's walk to our companions' car and get away from..." A jet drowned out his voice. When they reached the car, Joe looked through Frank's high power telescope, set on its low tripod. It was focused on the farm house. The only movement was a young rabbit chewing. He swung the scope about to where the shots originated. There was no sign of the truck.

"Might as well pack up and get..." another jet fractured the sky above. "Poor Frank and Darin, having to stake out that house. They must be half deaf by now. I'm surprised the vibration didn't destroyed that farm house long ago," Heather said. "Now can we open the letter?"

Joe pulled off the road and stopped. "Here," he said, "you may have the honor." She opened the envelope carefully and extracted a piece of heavy bond paper. She unfolded it while commenting on its quality, but fell silent after a moment, then handed it to Joe who read it aloud:

"My dear Mr. Jensen, if you're reading this, it is only because the sights on my rifle might have been a hair off. Well, another time, another place. Perhaps on home ground. Your demise is pending. P."

"Do you think he knows where we live, Joe?" Heather asked with, for her, a rare expression of fear.

They found a parking space close to the Drouot Galleries. As they approached the door, a man suddenly appeared in front of them. He wore a faded jacket with large pockets. On his head was a beret from which fell long, yellow hair in need of care. His eyes were hidden behind dark glasses. "Pardon, Monsieur, please look into my pocket, then do as I tell you."

The young man raised his hand slightly from his pocket, exposing a hand gun. Joe said calmly, "Before you do or say anything further, I suggest you walk away. Throw the gun in the Seine and find better work."

The young man froze at the calmness of Joe's voice. "Merci, Monsieur, I think you may be right." He turned and disappeared into the crowd of pedestrians.

Joe and Heather looked at each other and shrugged. "On such a nice day. He must be desperate," Heather said.

They stopped by the receptionist's desk and asked to see the person in charge of 19th century paintings. "Just a moment please and I'll see if he is available. You are...?" she asked.

"Jensen. Just tell him its about the Corot, the Italian landscape, and we can't wait." Joe said.

She pressed a couple of buttons and spoke softly into the phone. After hanging up, she turned to them and said, "If you would be kind enough to wait in the conference room, Monsieur Lapage will be with you shortly."

Lapage joined them almost immediately. He was a dapper man in an elegant light gray suit with matching tie. He wore a pince-nez with a dark gray ribbon that hung straight down emphasizing bony high cheek bones. His reddened face showed a recent close shave and a strong astringent. Strange chalk white teeth were revealed as he smiled. Bowing slightly, he introduced himself.

"Now Monsieur and Madame Jensen, how may I assist you?"

Heather favored him with a winning smile as Joe explained their interest. "It's about the Corot landscape your men picked up a few hours ago. We have a keen interest in it and want to know its provenance and the person who ordered its sale."

"Is something wrong with it? I have not personally had the opportunity to examine it yet. It has just arrived and..."

"No, Monsieur Lapage, I know the painting, and in my judgment it is right. You have, I trust, its history and its current owner, a James Chapman."

"Monsieur Jensen, you are well informed. The circumstances are a bit odd. This all happened late yesterday, just before closing. The owner insisted on signing the contract right then, as he was leaving the country that night—to where, he did not say. He gave us no address but asked that we hold the proceeds from the sale until he returned. As to its history, it was purchased from the artist by a man named Farquar, who was a farmer and the major land owner in the Sarcelles area. James Chapman bought the house and its contents about four years ago. May I ask, how recent was your viewing of the painting?"

"We were at the house when your men picked it up. It's a special canvas and should bring a record price."

"Let's hope so. Now, tell me, do you wish to place a reserve bid?"

"No, if possible, we'll be at the sale and place our bids then. We'll know better then our limit. We do thank you for your time and help."

Monsieur Lapage made his slight bow as he opened the door, "I hope to see you at the sale," he said, removing his pince-nez to watch Joe and Heather leave.

***

Joe and Heather were approaching the registration desk at the hotel when a deep voice from behind them said, "Got ya!"

Without turning, Joe said, "What took you so long? Any news on our shooter?"

"Long gone," Darin replied. "Cheeky bastard, he made off with the platform truck from a repair hanger and drove it around the edge of the airport just inside the fence. Here are a couple of the shells I found in the truck. You're lucky he didn't hit you. He had a lot of gun pointed your way."

"Yes, I know. It tore quite a hole in the house. He had a lot to consider at that distance, though—elevation, wind velocity..."

"Yes, Joe, and we can be grateful, because Palmer has a lot of talent when it comes to arms. He's as angry as a swarm of killer bees. Where are we going to pick him up this time?"

"Frank, you and Darin find a table in the cocktail lounge while H. and I check for messages. I'll join you in a moment and bring you up to date."

"Not Heather?"

"No, I want her to take care of a couple of things for me. We're going home."

"Nothing for you, Monsieur," the desk man said. "Is there anything else?"

"Yes, please reserve two tickets on the earliest flight to Washington, D.C., on the Concorde."

Joe walked Heather to the elevators, surveying the lobby as they walked. He asked her to call Karp and tell him what had happened, then pack. He would come up to take a shower in about fifteen minutes, after he had talked with Frank and Darin.

"We ordered you a tonic water with lime," Frank said.

"Thank you, that's just what I wanted." Joe brought them up to date on recent events, then showed them Palmer's note.

"He's a clever bastard. What timing! Looks like he's had his first go at you on his own. Perhaps he's run out of helpers. Now what?" Darin asked.

"From what he implies in the note about home grounds, I think it's best that H. and I get home and prepare a reception for him, just in case. We'll leave in a few hours, and I'd like you to follow. But first check the airports. Maybe we can find out where he's heading and when. If you catch him still in the air, report to Karp and with luck, a lot of luck, he can have him intercepted. When you know that he has left, return to D.C. and we'll meet at Robert's house. Is that agreeable?"

They both nodded. Joe looked at his watch. "I'm about due upstairs. Good hunting. See you in D.C." Before going upstairs, Joe stopped at the desk and asked to have more fresh bath towels delivered to their room. Then he bought a newspaper and stepped into the elevator with two couples. As he left the elevator, he saw the housekeeper approaching his door. She knocked and called, "Housekeeper." There was no answer. She knocked a second time and called a bit louder, "Housekeeper, your fresh towels." Joe arrived at the door in time to hear a male voice answer, "Just a moment. I'm not dressed. Just hand them to me through the door."

Joe took the towels from the housekeeper and motioned her to stay quiet and move away. The door opened and a bare arm extended to receive the towels. As the hand closed on them, Joe grasped the forearm and twisted it while slamming his shoulder into the door. There was a loud squeal of pain, and the figure slumped to the floor. Joe pushed into the room and closed the door behind him, stepping over the man's form. A small handgun lay on the floor close by, and

Joe kicked it across the room. He found Heather gagged, stretched out on the bed, her hands and feet tied. He pulled the towel from her mouth and untied her. "Take care of the man while I page Darin and Frank. I hope they're still in the bar."

Heather walked quickly to the door. "Get up and sit in the chair, now!" The young man got to his knees, then with the help of the wall, managed to gain his feet and walked slowly to the chair, supporting his arm. The young man was clearly in pain. Joe had dislocated his shoulder. "Fix it, please fix it! Pull it back in place," he pleaded.

"In good time," Heather said. She looked at Joe and smiled. "I was snookered. As I came in and passed the bathroom door, he zapped me. I have a lump on my head you wouldn't believe. Get our friends?"

"On the way. Did he molest you in any way?"

"No, when I came to, he was sitting in the chair with his gun pointing at the door, waiting for you. Remember him at the entrance of the Drouot Galleries?"

"Oh yes, I remember. The fellow with the gun in his pocket. Apparently he didn't take our advice. Well, friend, you want to tell us about it in a nice, orderly way, or...? Have you ever had two dislocated shoulders at the same time?"

"Fix it—pull it into place and I'll tell you," the young man said as he slumped deeper into the chair.

"Talk!"

Their eyes met and he began his story.

"I am called Mashell, Andre Mashell." His ashen lean oval face expressed a fear that the price of failure was to be paid. His hands quivered uncontrollably. "I drive a taxi now and then. Well, there was a fellow I met who asked me if I had ever killed anyone. I had been drinking, and I was feeling very good, so I lied and said, yes, three or four times, while in the army. Then he offered me ten thousand francs to kill you. He described you in detail and said you and Madame would be going to visit the Dourot Auction Gallery and that you were staying at the Maurice Hotel. I wanted to look you over, so I waited at the gallery. You looked easy, and I thought you were acting tough to impress your lady. The fellow gave me the money in advance and told me he would take it back if I didn't kill you. He didn't care whether your wife died or not. At the hotel I called on the house phone and got your room number. Then I waited until your lady arrived alone and hit her with a leather covered lead sap. Then the housekeeper came, and you surprised me. Now please pull my arm..."

There was a heavy knock on the door and Heather opened it to admit Frank and Darin.

"What have you here?" Darin asked.

Andre Mashell asked, "Who are you? What did I get myself into? Are you police or something like that?" Joe said, "Yes, something like that." After Darin and Frank heard what had happened, Frank said, "When you hit Mrs. Jensen on the head, you made the mistake of your life, fellow."

"Relax Frank, I'll survive. Darin, put his shoulder back where it belongs and take him for a ride. We have to catch a plane, and I think Joe wants to shower," Heather said. And to herself she added, "And I want to join him."

***

Joe paid their bill and was handed two tickets for the Concorde flight to Washington, D.C., that would depart from the Charles deGaulle Airport within two hours. It was a tight schedule, for they had to return the rental car to Le Bourget and shuttle to the deGaulle, check in, and hope the gate was close by.

Frank and Darin split up after delivering Andre Mashell to Karp's men in Paris. Frank visited security at Orly airport while Darin covered the de Gaulle and Le Bourget in hopes of finding Palmer's destination. They would fax any results to Robert. As they left on their appointed quests, the skies became gray and a light drizzle began to fall. Paris was once again a gray city that, as always, retained its charm.

"We made it with a minute to spare," Heather said as they pulled the safety belts tight.

Joe leaned over and kissed her and held her hand. "How's your head feeling by now?"

"It's fine. The throbbing has stopped. But my pride still hurts—letting him catch me off guard like that! If I hadn't been thinking of sharing the shower with you, it might have been different. It was lucky the housekeeper delivered the towels just then."

"Well, it told me what my life is worth to a sometime taxi driver."

The Concorde moved slowly out onto the runway, stood brooding a moment, then roared as it gathered speed, soon to soar like a great bird into the leaden sky. Moments later it broke free into the deep blue and began to race the sun as it headed west.

The seat belt sign was turned off, and they reclined their seats. Joe said, "Sweetheart, I've been thinking for some time about changing the location of my studio. It would be in some ways a drastic change, and I would do it only with your full agreement. We own a beautiful piece of land a few miles north of Dallas with a fair-sized lake, rolling hills, and pastures. There's a deep creek and old timber, pecan, oaks, elms, and many other kinds of trees. It's just far enough from the city so we won't have to become trapped in social activities or cultural politics. I was thinking of building a studio and home there. We could design it together. The climate is warmer and the days longer. What we give up may be little compared to what we would gain. Does this appeal to you?"

"My love, you certainly know how to win my heart. I didn't think any place like that was still available anywhere in the world. I could have a small studio of my own, to write. When can we visit it and start building?"

"As soon as we secure the home front. I want to move my work and certain things of value as soon as possible, before Palmer visits us."

"Do you think he really knows our address, or just Robert's?"

"He may not think about it, but I'm listed in Who's Who, and that gives the address. Then, too, he could get it from one of the galleries that represents me. I must call them—hope it's not too late to stop them from giving it out. He could also get the address from a museum, or from subscription lists for art magazines. We can only assume that he already knows, or soon will."

"No privacy, no escape anymore. I agree it's only a question of time, depending on what part of the world he fled to."

"Well, in the meantime let's dream of building our new nest in a warmer, friendlier climate."

The plane gently touched the wet runway. A light, drifting snow created multi-arching patterns across the hard surface as the Concorde sought its gate. Joe and Heather entered the airport, to be greeted by the happy voice of Robert. "Hi! You made good time! Give me a hug and kiss, sister-in-law. Joe, I'm glad you brought her home in one piece. And you, I hear that you just missed having a hole through you."

Joe held up his thumb and index finger to express the distance by which the bullet missed its mark. As they headed for Robert's car, Joe asked if there was any news yet concerning Palmer.

"Not yet. Perhaps something will have arrived by the time we get home. Rose has prepared a special dinner to celebrate your return, and there's a chance that Karp may join us. And you, Heather, I understand you let some young, would-be-killer clobber you. How was it? I don't mean to make light of it."

"I understand, Robert. Even the best of us get it once in a while. I confess my mind was focused on something quite different at the time."

"And may I ask what that was?"

"No, you may not."

Their spirits were high as they left the shelter of the terminal. A cold, bitter wind swirled about them as they ran for the car.

"Watch your footing, there are icy spots under the snow," Robert warned.

"How long has this been going on?" Joe asked.

"Just started last night. It was so nice two days ago that I took the boat out with Kathryn for most of the day. It was marvelous sailing," Robert sighed, remembering.

"Are we at last to meet her at dinner tonight?" Heather asked.

"She was invited, of course, but declined because she had to fly to Chicago for a few days. When she gets back..."

"I suspect she doesn't want to meet us. Did you tell her what we do?" Joe asked.

"Only that you're a painter and Heather is a poet, and once in a while you do some special work for the government. I didn't want the subject to dominate our conversations for days. I'd much rather discuss our possible future together."

"I understand, Robert. Some men just know how to woo a lady," Heather said, jabbing Joe in the ribs.

"Well, here we are. I have a nice fire waiting. After you've freshened up, we'll enjoy a drink before dinner. Mind the ice on the steps. I'll put the car away."

As they closed the front door behind them, a voice from the kitchen called, "Who's there?"

"Rose, it's Joe and Heather. Your kitchen smells wonderful. Come give us a hug." They met halfway. Heather visited with Rose while Joe checked the fax machine for recent messages. It was signaling the start of another message as he entered the study. When it shut down, Joe picked up the message: "Palmer left Aeroport d'Orly, Flight 617-7:15 for Boston. Too late to intercept at destination. We are on our way to Boston. Will call." It was initialed "F-D". He set it aside and joined Heather and Rose.

Robert entered the back door. "You still here? Thought you'd be upstairs."

"I was just telling Rose we've missed her and her cooking. French cuisine has nothing to better hers. But we'll go. See you later, Rose," Heather said. She took Joe's arm and led the way upstairs.

A quarter of an hour later they returned downstairs to find Robert and Karp standing by the fireplace. Karp was saying, "Please don't take offense, but my interest is yours, and I thought it would assure you to know."

"Good to see you, Karp," Joe said. Heather gave him a kiss.

"Know what? May I ask? Secrets?"

"No," Robert said. "Karp thinks I'm so smitten that I may overlook some of the qualities I sense in Kathryn."

"Such as?" Joe asked.

Karp replied, "I was telling Robert that I took it upon myself to check on her as I would anyone who gets close to our people and may have an influence on them. Well, it turns out she's triple-A. I was encouraging him to pursue the courtship and refused to tell him my findings. In time he'll know from her, and it will be better than my telling him."

"Karp, you're a romantic," Heather said, kissing him again. "What we want to know is when are we going to meet her? We haven't even seen a photograph. We only see the light in Robert's eye."

After dinner, as was his custom, Karp visited Rose and gave her a token gift. This time it was a simple, elegant, gold wristwatch engraved on its back: "To Rose. Karp, with love," with the date. She had given up trying to refuse such gifts. She was a happy lady who knew her love was returned.

"So now, somewhere in Boston, Palmer is most likely finding your address. Soon he'll have your studio cased, photographed, and staked out. It will take him a few days to set up, but it won't be long. What do you plan to do about it, Joe?" Karp asked.

"H. and I talked about it on the flight back. Some years ago I bought some acreage a bit north of Dallas with the idea of building a studio and home. This may be the time for it. We'll go to the studio in New York early tomorrow and move out the things of value to us. We'll store them for shipment to Dallas, leaving just the necessities for comfortable living. Then we'll set up defenses and a few offensive surprises and hope that this time Palmer himself appears. Darin and Frank should arrive late tomorrow, and they'll join us as shadows. My concern is the neighbors. Palmer is quite capable of blowing up the whole block to get us. Or he could just pick a spot and wait all by himself. And what he shoots, a protective vest won't slow down."

"That's all very well, but what I can't understand is why you refuse to kill him. You have the skills to split a hair at three hundred feet—you can match or out-match him. Why?" Karp asked.

"You know how I feel about killing, and the idea of destroying life is repugnant to me. It's against all my sensibilities. I could do so, but would only in the most desperate circumstances. But enough of this," Joe said. "There's more productive work to prepare for."

For the next few hours they theorized about events past, present, and future, sharing ideas about how it might be possible for Palmer to get the edge. All in all, it looked like the odds were stacked in his favor.

"What if it were like the old western days, when we'd meet out on the street at high noon so that neither of us would have the advantage of the sun. Can't you see Palmer and me squaring off for the quick draw..."

"No, I can only see him in a dark alley or on a balcony, back-shooting. Those days are long gone, if they ever existed. Dishonest men are basically cowards who are protected by a lack of conscience. Do you agree, Joe?" Karp asked.

"Of course you're right. It's part of the old children's story that says, 'I am just as big for me as you are big for you." Or I suppose my conscience is as guilt-free as yours. It's only after someone is caught that he may say, 'I guess I was wrong.' However, in the end, we have to live with ourselves, and what could be worse than losing one's own self respect?"

Karp stood up and said, "Well, dear friends, it's time for me to get back to the armory, and you all need to get to bed. It will be a long day tomorrow. Glad to see you back. Robert, catch your bird and nest her."

As they said their good nights, the last red ember fell through the grate and slowly turned to gray ash.

***

The morning came all too soon. Joe stirred, and Heather said, "Don't leave, I've got an idea."

Joe kissed her and said, "No ideas. Get up. We have to get home by eight, you lazy wench. Out! It's shower time."

"Well, why didn't you say so." She threw the blankets back and raised her nude body from the warm bed. "I'll adjust the water," she called.

Joe marveled to himself, "God, what a woman, and she's mine."

As they dressed, the weather report announced that the cold front was moving out to sea and the sun would break through by ten o'clock. The high would be in the middle-forties, the low twenty-eight.

Joe had called for the shuttle to pick them up, so as not to disturb Robert. As they descended the stairs, Rose greeted them with cups of coffee and a good-morning smile.

"Take a moment and enjoy your coffee. Will you be returning soon?"

"We hope so, but at the moment, we have no idea when. And again, thank you, Rose, for the special dinner. As always, it was appreciated," Heather said, kissing her.

"Come on, H., the shuttle is here. Swallow your coffee and let's get going. 'Bye, Rose, we'll keep in touch."

As they approached the airport shuttle, Joe hesitated a moment, shifting the fully packed small suitcase to his other hand. Heather lost a step beside him. He whispered, "It's wrong."

The driver held the door open for them. He wore a green jumpsuit and a visor cap. Long blonde hair covered his thick neck. He extended a large strong hand. "May I take your bag, sir?"

"No, it's not heavy. Are we alone, or are you picking up other passengers?" Joe asked, as he surveyed both the driver and his seat area.

"Just one more, not far from here, about two blocks." The driver closed the door and got behind the wheel.

They studied the driver but saw no signs of nervousness. He appeared most relaxed. Could Joe be wrong? Perhaps Palmer was getting to them. There was no way he could have set something up with this shuttle. Why did he sense the vehicle itself was wrong, Joe wondered. It was the color. Good God, he thought, he was becoming paranoid. He lowered the window a couple of inches, wetted a finger and rubbed it on the outer paint surface. The driver noticed Joe's actions, and his neck muscles tightened.

Joe's finger showed a strong orange color. It was a water-base casein that hadn't set long enough.

The shuttle stopped to pick up a lone male passenger. The door opened to admit a lone man wearing an off-the-rack ill fitting suit. A felt brimmed hat lowered to shield his eyes. He was similar in size to the driver. He carried no luggage. He opened the door himself and sat next to the driver. Good mornings were exchanged, and the shuttle drove on. A few words were spoken between the driver and his new passenger. There was little activity on the street as the driver pulled over to stop. The slow movement of the passenger did not go unnoticed. He turned to face Joe and Heather, holding a small hand gun. As he started to say, "This is a hold-up," the suitcase hit the gun, which went off, and then Joe's fist collided with the man's nose. Heather's hand found a nerve in the driver's neck, and he went limp. The passenger dropped the gun and covered his face with both hands. Joe and Heather pulled both men from the van and set them on the curb. Then they drove off. They had a plane to catch.

***

They left the van in a no-parking area, knowing that it would be spotted soon, ticketed, towed away, and discovered to have been stolen. They didn't have much time to reach their gate, so it was not until they were strapped in their seats that Heather said, "Joe, are we magnetic or something, that these things keep happening to us?"

"No, it's just the luck of the draw. That pair, in all probability, spent days planning a new kind of heist. Stealing and painting the van, having a friend at the airport to intercept the call and passing it on in time to get them moving, dropping a man off just far enough away to make it look legit...

"Let's hope we were their first victims. If so, and if they're smart, we were certainly their last. You know, we're carrying a few more grams of weight. The gun left a bit of lead in our laundry."

"Guess we should have made them pay for damages to the suitcase and our clothes."

Joe laughed. "They will, but not to us. The doctor bill will just about square it. It's strange, hitting a man in the nose doesn't hurt the fist nearly as much as hitting him on the jaw, and it's a lot more effective. I must remember to tell Robert."

***

From the plane Joe called the superintendent of his building to let him know they were returning and to inquire if everything was in order. He was assured it was and that only yesterday the super had watered the house plants and checked the temperature and humidity.

The flight from D.C. to LaGuardia seemed shorter this time. The plane seemed barely to have reached its assigned ceiling before it started its descent. Joe and Heather stopped for a leisurely breakfast in the airport coffee shop while talking further about moving to Texas. Joe cautioned that their main priority at the moment was to resolve the Palmer problem. They should not become sidetracked by dreams of their new home. They must, if possible, anticipate Palmer's next move, and to do so, they must know their neighborhood better. Joe was anxious to remove Robert's house as a target. The lease on Joe's studio had a little more than a year to run, which would allow ample time and flexibility to create his new plans. He felt responsible for the safety of his neighbors, few of whom he knew.

At most they felt it would take Palmer three days to find their address, for Joe had an unlisted phone number. They would try to put things together in a day and a half. They felt sure Palmer himself would case the neighborhood and watch their movements for a few days. Then if possible, he would hire backup support until he had the right time and place to make his kill. He was the hunter waiting in his blind, waiting for his trophy kill. The thought was not pleasant. Nevertheless knowing evened the situation a bit.

After arriving home, Joe went into the studio, as was his habit, to assure himself that it was in order. His pallet seemed to be seeking the fresh pigment that it had been deprived of for so long. The familiar studio odor still held, though, however faint. To the painter its fragrance was sweeter than the garden. Joe felt an urge to open a tube of cadmium red and enter a small dab into a white, but other things must be done first.

As he punched numbers on the phone, Heather called from the bedroom, "Joe, come look what that little bullet did to our underwear and your shirts."

"In a moment. I'm on the phone. Hello, yes. Joe Jensen. I need another number for a fax. Can you supply the fax as well? Good. It's most important I have it today. This morning if possible."

Joe finished his call, then joined Heather, who was holding up some holey clothes. She dropped the lead from a 32 caliber bullet into his hand. "So that's why you insisted on holding the suitcase on your lap. I marvel at you."

"I marvel at myself! Not often, just now and then. There was something strange about that van's color that didn't belong. Well, that's past. I've ordered a fax machine to communicate more easily with Karp and Robert and to receive messages, photos, and plans if we're out. While you go buy a week's provisions for the kitchen and have them delivered, I'll call Robert. I hope Frank and Darin are available. I want them to borrow some equipment from Karp and bring it with them."

"I'll go right now. Shall I plan on feeding our comrades, as well, to be safe?"

"Yes, and remember Darin's appetite."

"How could I forget?" Heather blew Joe a kiss and left.

Joe called a friend at the city planning department and asked him to prepare a printout on the immediately neighboring buildings and their occupants. He also asked him for the garbage pickup schedules. His friend said, "I suppose you want it yesterday."

"No," Joe said, "I want it sooner than that. I'll call you back with a fax number in a few hours."

Joe's next call was to Robert, who was in a happy mood. Kathryn was returning tomorrow, and he would take Karp's advice and pop the question if the right moment arose. But, he asked Joe, how would he know if it was the right moment? Joe's answer was not helpful at all. "You'll know. Don't think about it," he said. Robert then reported that Frank had called in looking for Joe. "He'll call you any time now. I told him you and Heather left early this morning."

Joe soon rang off, in case Frank might call. While waiting, he returned to the studio and selected a stretched canvas, which he placed on the easel. Its blank surface was inviting. He knew what he wanted to do, for he had several sketches containing first thoughts for it on the nearby drawing table. Unfortunately, this was not the time to set his pallet, however. He found himself mouthing seldom-spoken adjectives describing his feeling for Palmer.

The phone rang, interrupting his unkind thoughts of the enemy. As he picked up the phone, there was a knock at the door. A voice said, "fax man."

It was Frank on the phone. "Hold a moment Frank. I'll be just a moment, the fax man just arrived."

Joe opened the door and nodded at the new arrival. "That was quick," he said motioning him in and pointing where he wanted it placed.

"I'm on the phone. Please do what's needed," Joe said as he returned to the phone.

"O.K. Frank, any luck in Boston?" Joe asked.

"No, not much. He took the red-eye to New York and should be there by now. Looks like he'll do his research there."

"OK, pick up a package for me from Karp and join us as soon as possible. This could move faster than I had expected. See you both soon."

A key turned in the lock, and the door kicked open. Heather's happy voice shouted, "We're here! "

"Good, need a hand?"

"No, we can manage. Have you heard from Frank or Darin?"

"Yes, I'll bring you up to date as soon as the phone man is through. Then we have some scouting to do about the neighborhood. When will the groceries be delivered?"

"They should be on their way now. The grocer says hello, and he's glad you're back. I paid him by check, though he offered to put it on your account. He likes the idea that you owe him, I guess."

"No, he's afraid I may start doing business with his competitor. I wouldn't, but we get better service this way."

"All ready to go, Mr. Jensen. Checks out fine. Just sign here. Thanks. Your new number is on the invoice. Let us know when we can be of further service."

Joe thanked him and showed him out. He then called his friend at city planning to give him the number so that he could fax the requested information and drawings.

"You may not believe this, Joe, but not long after your call, a fellow came in and asked for the identical information about your neighborhood that you wanted. I had it set aside, waiting for a fax number, to send it to you.

"I convinced him that he had to get a letter from another office before I could let him see it. He wasn't happy, but said he'd be back. Told me to get the information together. He got really angry when I insisted on seeing some authorization first. What the hell's up?"

"First," Joe said, "start sending it now." He gave the number, and within a minute the fax bell indicated that a message was about to be transmitted. In the meantime, Joe described Palmer and told his friend that Palmer was wanted for several murders. He advised him to have the police or security guards to hold him if he returned. He advised the greatest possible caution.

"Yes, that sounds like the man who was here. He looked more like a bookkeeper, though. Are you sure he's..."

"Yes, I'm sure. He's about as harmless as a stepped-on rattlesnake. I can't warn you enough, my friend. He's foxy. He probably won't return, but will send someone else. Where else could he get information of that kind?"

"He could see it in the tax plat books, but he'd have to take notes in the sight of a clerk. The books are so large and heavy, it takes a special photocopy machine to handle them. I'm faxing two more sheets, and then you'll have all the information there is. And thanks for the warning, Joe. Don't forget to call me when you can and tell me what this is all about."

Joe turned to Heather. "H., we have a lot to learn about our neighbors, and we have to do it quickly. The fax sheets will give us the layout of each building and who lives there. Wherever and whenever possible, we'll talk to someone in each building and find out if any of the apartments or duplexes are empty, how long, if anyone is out of town, and so forth. You know what we're after—access to roofs, dumbwaiters, basements, spaces between buildings."

"I understand," Heather said. "I've done it all before. The de Gaulle assassination attempt, remember?"

"That was Paris, not Queens, New York, but the modus operandi should be about the same. The killer was disguised as an old man with a crutch, false beard, patch over one eye, who walked into a house past several police who knew there was to be an attempt on the President's life. He boldly let himself into a private house, killed a couple of women without a sound, and climbed the stairs to the second floor to gain access to front rooms. He stationed himself in a bay window, where he dismantled the crutch and removed the stock, magazine, and high-power scope from under his coat. He had a clear shot at his target."

"Yes, I remember. It was only by chance that the daughter returned home and found her mother dead. Her screams brought the gendarmes, who arrived just as the assassin pulled the trigger. His shot was said to strike the cobblestones between de Gaulle's feet."

"Yes, my love. I suspect our friend Palmer may have played a part in that plot."

"How can we warn the neighbors without scaring them out of their wits, Joe?"

"We can't. It will be up to us to just take care of things. We must become acquainted with everything and everyone. Damn, I wish Frank and Darin were here. You take this side, I'll take the other. Good luck, H."

Joe's studio had a large window that faced directly north, an exposure preferred by painters for the constant light it offered throughout the year. It occupied the top floor of an old red brick duplex. His landlord lived directly beneath him, and a Korean family of six rented the first floor. The two halves of the duplex were separated by a solid wall broken by an octagonal light well. The second half was occupied by families of three or four different nationalities. The super who took care of the building lived in the basement apartment alone. His wife had died of cancer two years before. There was a sheltered staircase at the back of the building that served as both fire escape and access to the carport and alley.

In general, this was typical of the design of the buildings on both sides of the street, with different colored bricks and varying entrance designs. The one exceptional feature was the studio window, which Joe had put it at his own expense. Anyone who looked up would surmise that the space was occupied by an artist. Under the present circumstances the skylight was a flag for the hunter.

Joe and Heather found their neighbors most courteous and willing to answer their questions. Almost all of them invited their visitor in for tea or coffee to become better acquainted. It was, at times, difficult to get away.

The neighbors said they would, of course, be happy to report anyone who looked out of place or was new. There was a strong sense of neighborhood pride, and Joe and Heather were pressed to promise to join the spring block party. There were no vacancies in the whole area.

As Heather crossed the street to return to the studio, a cab pulled up and discharged Frank and Darin, who unloaded four good-sized boxes.

"Well, well, we have a welcoming committee. How about that. Where's Joe? Is he painting while you walk the streets?"

"Now Darin, watch your tongue or you'll get no supper."

"Sorry, H., please forgive me. A growing boy needs his supper."

After paying the driver, Frank said, "Good to see you, Heather. Is Darin giving you trouble? I told you he was no good. Want me to punch him out?"

"This is a respectable neighborhood, guys. No street fighting. Wait till you get upstairs. By the look of those boxes, by the time you get them up to the studio, all the fight will be out of both of you." She kissed them both and they happily carried their burden up three flights.

Joe had not returned. Heather put the kettle on to heat water for coffee and filled a bowl with bagels. They sat around the kitchen table and she told them what she and Joe had done since their last meeting. The coffee was made and the bagels diminished a bit by the time Joe arrived.

"Well now," Joe said, "here I come home to find my wife entertaining two strange men in the kitchen."

Darin tossed him a bagel. "Dunk a bagel, Joe. Heather is telling us what you've been up to. I like the airport shuttle bandits story, but I don't understand that color stuff."

"Elementary, my dear Darin. You see, it was a new model van, and they had wanted to change its color quickly. To have it dry fast, they used a casein paint, which has a cheese base as a binder. What they didn't take into account was that although it did dry quickly, it had a dull, matte finish. When have you seen a new car or van that wasn't pridefully polished to a high gloss?"

"And that's what told you the driver was going to rob you?" Frank said. "Well, I'll be..."

Joe smiled, "Not exactly, it just made me suspicious enough to be on guard."

"That was sharp. I doubt that many would have caught that," Darin said. "What's your feeling on Palmer? Will he try to get close to you, hand-to-hand, you know? Or will he become the sniper again?"

"I really think he'll be as far away as possible. He removed the element of surprise when he left his note. Most likely he's regretted it since. His misguided ego and his anger have gotten in his way. One stupid move was enough for him. I don't look for another. Well, let's see what you brought with you in the boxes."

"What you asked Karp for, plus one or two things he added on his own," Frank said.

"Let's look and get things set up as quickly as possible. It's going to take time, and knowing he's in the city gives us a day or two." As Joe spoke, a helicopter flew over very slowly. They could see it from the studio window.

"The bastard, the bloody bastard!" Darin exclaimed. The rest of them just stared as the copter dipped its nose and disappeared from sight.

Heather said only, "He knows."

"That's a move I didn't expect. That's something else, getting a pilot to fly that low over the city. Maybe he was holding a gun on him. That move could be worth his license. Let's get with it," Joe said.

The helicopter made two more passes that brought many of the neighbors out to see what was happening. With each pass it would hover and slowly make a full turn about twenty feet above the roofs. Its downdraft blew surviving snow from shadowed corners, showering it on the street.

From a vantage point by the studio window Joe watched through field glasses. They brought the pilot and his passenger in focus so closely that he felt he could almost touch them. On the pilot's jacket he read the name, Hemmings. The second man was using a video camera. It was not Palmer.

Joe called to Heather. "Call the Port Authority and check on a pilot named Hemmings and where he parks his chopper. Its number is HP744NY. I'll fax Karp."

It took Heather ten minutes to get through the Port Authority's numerous departments before she made contact with someone who could give her the information. It had one of those aggrevating efficient mechanical systems where a recorded voice informs you to press one if you want such a department, two, three, etc. After announcing each in turn it suggests that you press nine and hold until an operator responds. Joe had left to help Frank and Darin mount sensors about the neighborhood, so after writing a note, she left for the airport. She went down the back stairs to the carport, hoping to see one of them, but they were still out. All was quiet. The residential streets had little traffic, and her departure went unnoticed.

On the other side of the runways, far from the main terminal of La Guardia, were the hangars that served the private and corporate aircraft. The road leading to them ended at a guard gate, where a uniformed guard asked Heather to show her pass. He was a smartly dressed man in his late fifties whose smile revealed a firm, yet gentle nature. His posture gave evidence of having served in the armed forces.

"Sorry, I have no pass. I'm looking for a Mr. Hemmings. The Port Authority told me I might find him here. Do you know him?" Heather asked.

"Yes, indeed. Fine gentleman, keeps his whirlybird and offices in hangar 3." The guard handed Heather a clipboard. "Please sign in, Miss, and put the time. How long will you be?"

"Not long if I find him right off You sure he's still here?"

"Yes, quite sure. We usually exchange a few words or a joke before he leaves."

As the guard talked, Heather read the list of names without recognizing any of them other than Hemmings'. She noted the names on either side of his, but the times marked didn't jibe. Hemmings had arrived alone. She returned the clipboard, and the guard waved her through. "OK, Mrs. Jensen. Hangar 3 is over there. I'll see you on your way out."

She drove around the back side of the hangar and pulled in, stopping between freshly painted white lines before a door with a large 3 on it. Inside she counted six helicopters parked within their rectangular yellow markings. She approached a mechanic who was adjusting a carburetor on a movable bench.

"Pardon me, could you tell me where I might find Mr. Hemmings?"

Without looking up the mechanic said, "In his office, second door, far wall to your right, lady." He seemed totally occupied knowing that if he looked up he would be involved in conversation that might cost time he could not afford. A promised deadline had to be kept.

"Thank you." On the way she checked the numbers on the parked choppers.

As she approached the office door she noted its glass panel was closed off by a shade. Her knock went unanswered. She turned the knob and opened the door. The room was small, about 12 by 18 feet. Against the far wall was a row of old green filing cabinets stacked with books, magazines, and model planes. The other walls were hung with numerous photos of pilots and helicopters. Across the simple, blond wood desk that faced the door lay the limp figure of Mr. Hemmings, his left arm stretched out across the desk top, fingers spread as if trying to reach something. His head lay on its side, eyes wide open. A black hole with a red rim made a third eye in his forehead. His right arm hung down, just touching the floor. A few inches away lay a hundred dollar bill folded into the shape of a toy airplane. Nothing seemed out of place or disturbed.

Heather left the office, closing the door behind her. She wiped her prints off the knob. The mechanic was still working as she approached him.

"Pardon me, sir, sorry to interrupt you again, but you seem to be the only one here. Could you tell me if anyone left the hangar in the last several minutes?"

"Not lately, lady. The last one I saw was Billy Bun."

"Who is Billy Bun?" Heather asked.

"He's a photographer who works with the pilots on commission."

"When you saw him last, did he have a video camera with him?"

"Yes, I believe so. Yeah, I'm sure he did. He said hello to me as he left—mmm, I think it was about half an hour ago."

"Would he have left by the guard gate to sign out?"

"Not necessarily. He has the run of the place. He could drive one of the airport cars over to the main terminal."

"Thanks very much. Mr.—ah, McCain." Heather noted the name on his coveralls. He nodded and continued working.

On the way out, Heather stopped at the guard gate to sign out.

"Well, did you see Hemmings? Nice fellow. Very popular around here."

"No, his door was closed and the shade was pulled. He didn't answer to my knock, so I guess he may be flying. I'll be back or call him later."

"I'll look for you, miss."

"Before I leave, tell me, do you know a Billy Bun?" Heather asked.

"The photographer, yes. I see him now and then, but not today. Mostly he comes across from the main terminal. You need some photos done? I have some of his cards here. Let me give you one." The guard opened a drawer and thumbed through a stack of business cards.

"Ah! Here it is." He handed the card to Heather. She thanked him and drove off.

***

"What else can we do to spot our man before he spots you, Joe?" Frank asked as they returned to the studio.

"I think I'll let him shoot me, how about that?" Joe said.

"You've gone bonkers," Darin said.

"No, what I mean is..."

"Hello! Hello, I'm back," Heather said as she came in from the kitchen. "You miss me?"

"We just arrived ourselves. Where have you been?" Joe asked.

"Following up on the helicopter pilot, Hemmings, and his photographer friend, Billy Bun."

"Billy Bun! Where did you find a Billy Bun?" asked Darin.

Heather told of her outing and detailed the position of the body, hoping it would mean something to Joe.

"How sad it is to have so many die because one man wants to kill me. Palmer truly is eaten with hatred and revenge. For once in his life he's paying and not profiting by his own rules. These cat and mouse games are out of character. He chases us, we chase him..."

"I'm sure we all agree with you, Joe. Wouldn't you think he'd take his money and retire to some remote place in the world?" Heather said.

"How do you figure the Hemmings killing, Joe?" Frank asked.

"I don't think the photographer, Billy Bun, did it. What little H. said about him leads me to believe that Palmer came in and left with him. If Bun had shot his friend, he probably would have aimed for the torso, the heart. Only a very self-assured pro would place his shot in the forehead, between the eyes. Palmer most likely didn't have the money he'd promised them, and he's not the kind of man to argue. I fear for Billy Bun! He probably took Palmer out through the main terminal with the video film. He's most likely looking at it at this moment in a hotel not too far away."

"When do you think he'll make his move, and how?" Heather asked.

"That's the big question. First, he'll go over the film several times, make diagrams and plot three or four ways to approach the target. That's me. He'll have to find and buy or steal what arms or explosives he'll require, and that may take him several days unless he has connections here. The Heavenly Mortuary, if it's still in business, won't help him. The Embassy delegation would be glad to see him, but not for the reasons he may wish for. There's the possibility that we might leave—that would give him fits. And that may be a good idea. Let's give that some thought. H., who lives directly across the street from us on the second and third floors?"

Heather left to get her clipboard and Frank said, "I think I know what you have in mind. Palmer isn't going to leave without hurting you in some way. He could lob a mortar shell from a block or two away."

"It crossed my mind. That and a dozen other things he could do. He could find another chopper and use a bazooka and blow the studio apart. That's one of the reasons I removed everything of personal and real value."

"Here's the list, Joe. On the second floor are the Rosequests and their son, who attends PS 69. The third floor is occupied by the Florries. They're a young working couple. The owner lives on the first floor with his son, Mark, a baseball player. You may know of him—Mark White? What do you have in mind, Joe?" Heather asked.

Joe ignored the question and asked, "Who are the arms dealers living in New York now? There must be at least a half dozen. Maybe Karp could put a bug in their ear about Palmer. H., give him a call. I'll go visit our neighbors across the street."

***

Giovanni was a squat-looking man. His bulbous nose and the fringe of hair that circled his bald pate gave him the appearance of a friar who had imbibed too many sacramental spirits. His heavy, black-framed glasses had quarter-inch thick lenses. At the moment he sat deep in an oversized cushioned chair in a dark corner. A red velour covered rope, supported by brass standards, kept visitors eight feet away.

A slight, neatly dressed man was ushered in and brought before the barrier by two tough wrestler-types who made the visitor look even smaller.

"He's clean. Want us to stay?" one of them asked.

"No, I'll ring when he's ready to leave." The soprano voice that came from Giovanni's thick lips was completely unexpected.

"Now, Mr. Potter—it is Potter, isn't it? You are interested in purchasing some hardware? Just what do you want that you think I can help you with?"

"First, Mr. Giovanni, may I thank you for seeing me. I know your time is valuable, and what I'm after may seem trivial, but at the moment my client wants to see if I can deliver."

"Ah, so you are an agent. If I had such hardware, where would you want it delivered?"

"Here. I can pick it up myself, if that's agreeable. I have a list. May I hand it to you, sir?"

"No! You stay on your side of the rope! Read it to me. I may not have what you want." His hand rested close to the call button. "I must warn you, Mr. Potter, my hardware is expensive, and I don't bargain. If that's agreeable, you may continue."

"Understood. I will pay on delivery. I trust that it will be quality goods and hope volume quantity will be available later."

"Mr. Potter, your people are planning a war?"

"Just a small one."

"Then read your list."

"I want a rocket launcher and six rockets; a machine pistol; twenty pounds of plastic explosive with timing caps; a rifle with scope, the largest caliber available; contact fuses; a remote-control plane just large enough to carry five pounds; and a half case of grenades."

"All this for demonstration...?"

"Yes."

The door opened and one of the guards entered. "Sorry to interrupt, sir, but there's a call you should take now. It's a man named..."

"No names! I'll take it. Excuse me, Mr. Potter. This will take but a minute." He reached into the shadow beside his chair and picked up a phone. "Giovanni," he said. His eyes remained focused on his guest, without changing expression. "Yes, yes, possible.

Yes, yes, I agree." The guard had moved close. Potter turned his ring about so that it was facing his palm. He parried the guard's arm and struck him in the neck. As the man fell, Potter ducked under the barrier rope and was upon the arms dealer before he could reach the alarm button. The needle scraped along Giovanni's heavy neck, and he was no more. Potter picked up the phone and tried to imitate the soprano voice of his victim, but the line was dead. He replaced the phone and pressed the button, then ducked into the darkness behind the chair. The second guard rushed in to find his partner limp on the floor and the boss slumped in his chair. He flung the standard aside and walked over the rope to check for signs of life. As he reached out to check Giovanni's pulse, he felt a prick on his neck and jumped backward. His mouth opened as his eyes closed. He was dead as he hit the floor. Potter's supply of poison was exhausted. He retrieved the pistols from his victims. A moment of panic seized him as he found the door locked. Not knowing who else might be close at hand, he turned his back and leaned against the wall to think. He smiled at the scene. A great arms dealer, so well protected, with his muscle-bound guards dead at his feet. The button. He must try it first before shooting the lock. He moved like a dancer across the room to the dead man's chair and pressed the alarm button. Nothing happened. Well, at least he knew no one was on the other side of the door. He pressed the button twice, and heard a click as the door opened. Now he was confronted with a new problem. Would he dare try another arms dealer? His options were all but closed. A gun collector—he would find a private collector and help himself! The catalogues would direct him.

Palmer left and closed the door behind him. A different kind of silence fell upon the room, only one that death knows.

***

"What did you think of your neighbor and his ball-player son?" Heather asked Joe when he returned.

"Well, not being a devotee of the game, I was hard put to keep up with them. The son was in a World Series, and I had to hear how his base hit brought in the winning run. It wasn't easy to press my point without revealing what was going on, but, in the end, they will be happy to cooperate, if need be. What about your call to Karp?"

"That Karp is something else. He had anticipated your idea about the arms dealers and was in the middle of his calls when I interrupted him. He had just been talking to a man named Giovanni, who actually had Palmer in the room, when the line suddenly went dead. Then a voice trying to imitate the dealer's strange soprano voice took over. Karp said he would call the police to investigate when we're finished. He suspects that there are a few bodies lying around. But now Palmer's sources are dried up. He'll have to find new ones. Karp feels that he may look for the major gun and weapons collectors next. He said he'd try to warn them to be on the alert. The police will cover the gun stores for the next few days."

Joe was silent for the next several minutes. Heather, Frank, and Darin left him alone in the studio while they went to the kitchen to discuss what they thought their next moves should be. This was done over coffee and the remaining bagels

Joe sat in a chair facing the blank canvas that challenged his brush to bring it to life, to give pleasure and solace to those who viewed it. He was deeply angry that a person such as Palmer could rob him of time he could be using to paint, creating something of lasting value. Reluctantly he acknowledged to himself that this time he would have to kill Palmer. He had to get close enough to kill without hesitation. He would have to respond as Palmer would, with his Arab terrorist training. At any hint of threat, strike first, don't wait to let your opponent make the first move. He must not let Palmer get within touching distance. Nor must he give him time to set up a weapon that would destroy the whole building and others around it. As he stared, the canvas began to take shape as if his brush were full of rich color and he was applying it to a welcoming surface. He was losing his concentration, so he turned his swivel chair around and closed his eyes. Palmer, Palmer. He must think only of Palmer, not of his growing hatred for this abominable person who possessed no conscience, who would kill or mutilate or destroy anything in his way. It was a full hour later before Joe joined his companions in the kitchen.

"Ah! Dear Holmes, did your meditation resolve anything?" Heather asked.

"Yes, dear wife, but I see that all the bagels are gone."

"Sorry, old boy. We were going over past events in an effort to anticipate what our friend Palmer would do next. He's agile and creative, but my feeling is that he's about to throw all caution aside and come head on without warning or tricks—just shooting as soon as he's within range. He may be disguised just enough to get a slight edge. He'll wear protection, so it will require a shot between the eyes to stop him. His neck will be covered, for he'll remember the dart that felled him the first time," Darin said.

"I forgive you for eating the last bagel. It helped your thinking. My thoughts were along the same track. H., Frank, what do you think?" Joe asked.

Heather looked at Frank. "Give, dear friend. You have other ideas."

"If he comes up empty trying to get heavy weapons, he may go out of town for them. But with Karp calling around, getting other agencies to check known sources, he may be unsuccessful. That will give us more time, but how much time, who can say? He will pick the time, and the place."

"I agree," Joe said. "H., what have you got to add?"

"For what it's worth, I think we should be trying to locate him. God only knows how many hotels and rooming houses there are in New York, plus bed-and-breakfasts. We should at least check the ones within a mile radius of the airport. There should still be a day or two before he makes his move. He'll continue to study the video film to know this neighborhood as if he lived here, so we can check places that have video capabilities. We can eliminate the ones in the area fairly quickly and visit the others. Joe, your friend at the city can do it on the computer and a printout can be faxed to us."

"Good thought. I'll call him right now. Anything else? If not, while I make the call, toast me a piece of pound cake with some butter and a cup of French roasted coffee, will you? Darin may watch me eat it."

"Make that for two," Darin said. "I can't stand to see a man eat alone. It'll give me an appetite."

"Then make that for three," Frank said.

"I think I'd best call for Rose to take care of you fellows if you're going to keep this up. To think Robert has her alone. I wonder how his romance is developing? Perhaps he does need Rose more than we," Heather said.

Joe returned. "We should have our answer in a few minutes. He asked me if I was aware that he worked for the city and that I now owed him two dinners. I told him that could get him in trouble, but I'd consider it."

"Come, eat your cake while you have a chance. Darin is within reach of it."

They spent the next half hour bringing everything into focus. The fax bell announced its incoming message. Frank volunteered to get it. When he returned, he said, "Not bad, there are only six hotels and five B and B's listed." He handed the fax to Joe.

"Good, very good. We'll divide them up and keep in touch with each other using intercoms. They're all within range. We need to announce exactly when we approach and leave an address. I'll drop you off at a point where they should be within walking distance. When they're not, take a cab. When you're finished, come back within a block or two of the studio and walk the neighborhood. Look for anything that may be out of place, or anyone. Darin, have you had enough fuel to last the trip?" Joe said.

"Come on now, you're going to give me a complex if you keep this up. Let's go." Darin held the kitchen door open and they filed out and down the back stairs to the carport.

Joe dropped Frank off at the airport hotel, then Darin a mile away. Before Heather left, he asked if she wanted him to join her, but she refused, saying there was no need, no danger. She doubted that she would be recognized if Palmer did see her alone. Joe kissed her as she left. "Look like a tourist," he said, "and..." She was gone.

Joe had one family-type motel and two bed-and-breakfasts to visit. The first had had no single male visitor for the past week or any single that fit the description of Palmer. The second B and B was just three blocks away from the studio. It was an old house, freshly painted white, with apple-green shutters. A wrought iron fence separated the sidewalk from a three-foot area that promised to be green grass when spring arrived. The double oak panel doors supported thick, etched glass with a floral design. An old-fashioned bell pull invited the hand with its polished surface. Joe felt himself in another time when he rang the bell. Its sound delighted the ear, as did the voice of the elderly lady who responded.

"Wipe your feet, young man, and come in from the chill."

"Yes, thank you, ma'am. It's a bit bitey, but there's a promise of an early spring. I'm Joe Jensen. I live just three blocks away."

"I am Mrs. Flowers," she said with pride, and proud she looked standing straight, permitting her floral pattern dress to reveal a trim figure. Her smile was as contagious as her sparkling eyes and voice. Not to like this lady would be difficult.

"And I am most happy to meet you, Mrs. Flowers."

"What can I do for you, young man? You need a room for the night, or one of my special dinners or breakfasts?"

"No, not at the moment, but maybe one day my lovely wife and I could be so honored. At the moment, I may need your help. We're looking for this man." Joe handed her a photo of Palmer.

"Oh my, that's Mr. Potter. He was here the night before last. Strange comings and goings. He left at two A. M. and returned just before four. He tried not to disturb anyone. What was most strange was that he didn't stay for my famous breakfast. Don't you think that peculiar, young man? What did you say your name was?"

"Just call me Joe. Tell me, did he have a videotape with him?"

"Why, yes, he did. After my husband and I went to bed, he used our VCR. In the parlor, you know. Strange, he looked and looked at the tape, but there was no sound, or else he had it turned way down."

"Anything else you remember about him?"

"Well, let's see," she said, closing her eyes to envision Mr. Potter. After a long pause she said, "Only that he carried a case like a violin case. Nothing else. Does that mean anything to you?"

"Could I ask a very special favor of you, Mrs. Flowers?"

"I suppose. You really will come for my famous breakfasts sometime?"

"Yes, and I'll send two of my friends. One of them eats like a horse and the other like a normal man. Now, if Mr. Potter returns, then leaves the house again at any hour, night or day, please call this number. Remember, call only after he leaves, and I'll take you and Mr. Flowers for a very elegant dinner. Promise?"

"I'll do that young man. I'd like to meet your Mrs." Joe kissed her on the cheek as he left, relishing both her blush and the expression on her face. He promised to come again for her famous breakfast.

***

The photographer waited in the airport car thinking how odd his assignment was shooting film from a helicopter of such a neighborhood at such an altitude. He knew it was against the law, but what the hell, it was good money, very good. It would save him from an angry landlord who threatened to evict him. He was apprehensive about the assignment, especially the man he was waiting for.

Billy Bun sat and warmed up the airport car while his employer settled accounts with Hemmings, his pilot friend. Before long, his man arrived and joined him, requesting that he drive to the far end of the runway instead of cutting across the field. Billy Bun said, "It can be pretty noisy at times."

"No problem. I have my reasons. Let's get going."

"You're the boss," Billy said. Beads of sweat began to form on his forehead. Something was wrong; his faint smile tried to hide a growing fear.

"How do you feel your film turned out?"

"I guarantee my work. Your money back if you don't like it. I take great pride in my work. I didn't ask before, but are you writing something about that neighborhood? I know it a little. It's well-established, clean. The people are mix of nationalities and colors. There's a pro baseball player, an orchestra conductor, and a painter of some reputation. You'll see footage of his studio. Lots of professional people. Should be a good supply of material squeezed into that small area."

"What's the painter's name?"

"I don't remember. His father was murdered a few years ago. A Senator, I believe."

"Hold your ears, a jet is coming in," Billy suggested.

"Stop a minute."

"Here? Why?" The beads of sweat began to run, producing streaks on his cheeks.

"Yes."

Billy Bun stopped and put the car into park. He glanced to his right and was amazed to see that his employer was holding a gun and motioning him to get out of his car. In shocked disbelief he opened the door and backed out. His throat went dry. "Why?" he asked. His only answer was the bullet that entered his forehead, spaced neatly between his eyes. The roar of the jet engines fell silent.

The car was found next to Gate One, the closest to the terminal lobby. The body of Billy Bun lay behind the jet windscreen, off the runway, in tall grass, waiting for the mower blades to find it.

***

Joe pulled the car into the carport. It was pick-up day, and the alley was neatly stacked with plastic bags by each house. He looked at his watch. If the trash men were on time, they should appear in about ten minutes. He walked casually down the alley to the far street, seeing neither cat nor mouse. Only the hum of distant traffic disturbed the calm. As he reached the end of the alley, Joe heard the shifting gears of the garbage truck. He stepped into the nearby carport, pressing his body against its wall. His hand went into his inner jacket and rested on the butt of his dart gun. The truck passed him and stopped when its back paralleled the neatly stacked plastic bags. Familiar faces jumped from the rear platform. Strong hands threw the bags into the open cavity, to be pushed and crunched forward into the huge steel cylinders. The truck passed on to retrieve the next pile.

Joe stood still, sensing an approaching presence. The truck was nearing the end of the alley when a figure appeared. Joe stepped forward, and the figure turned and fell to one knee with a gun pointing at him. He spread his arms wide and said, "Surely you don't want to get rid of me so soon?"

"Joe! You gave me a start. Are we getting trigger-happy?"

"No. Just looks like we're honed razor sharp. This may just be our edge."

"Well, love, let's get home and relax. A hot shower would help. Hope you had some luck. I didn't."

"Oh yes, I'll tell you about it when Frank and Darin get in. I did promise a lady I'd let her serve us a famous breakfast soon."

"What's that about?"

"Never mind now. Race you for the shower. Go, go."

Heather tripped him and raced on. "Foul! Foul!" Joe yelled, pretending to limp after her.

***

Neither Darin nor Frank was back yet. "How long do you think we have before they arrive?" Heather asked, with a glint in her eye.

"Just long enough," Joe said.

***

Forty minutes later, removing a freshly brewed pot of coffee from the stove, she called, "Joe," loud enough to reach the studio over the Chausson quartet. He was sitting, staring blankly at the inviting canvas again, thinking about Palmer. How strange the moment was, he mused. The love he felt for the most important person in all the world; the hate and the need to dispose of a man; the need to create. He found the juxtaposition of such thoughts troublesome, and so the coffee was particularly welcome at this time. As he left the studio, he heard a heavy knocking at the door. No doubt that was Frank and Darin. Joe opened the door. "You trying to rattle my door off its hinges?" Darin sniffed, "Step aside, I smell fresh coffee..."

"Only because you're bigger than I," Joe said. "Frank with you?"

"I'm coming, on my way." His voice drifted up from the floor below. "Just one more moment."

"What's he up to?" Joe asked.

"Oh, he's playing. He bought some pressure caps at a novelty shop and he's placing them under the carpet on the stairs, just in case."

"Won't the carpet muffle the sound?"

"I suppose, somewhat. Most likely it will burn a hole in the rug and give whoever steps on it a hot foot. But Frank will be Frank."

"Come on, fellows. Here's coffee, and I found some doughnuts Darin missed," Heather called.

The kitchen table seems to be the most used piece of furniture in a house. It's certainly the most used conference table anywhere. Joe reported his meeting with the B and B lady and his promise that they'd share one of her breakfasts. There was only a slight chance that Palmer would return there. Frank had found a similar B and B where Palmer had stayed and viewed the tape on their VCR. Darin had found two small hotels where he had checked in for a single night each. In walking the neighborhood they had found nothing suspicious or out of place, except for a tradesman who had visited with the super of their building.

"When was that?" Joe asked.

"While we were all out," Darin said.

Joe went to the phone and punched the intercom button. "Henry, this is Joe. Everything OK?"

"Yes, Mr. Jensen, no problem."

"I understand you had a visitor."

"Oh, yes, yes, that was my brother from St. Louis, Alfred. You need me for something?"

"Not really. We'll see you later." Joe hung up and said, "Let's go. The super's in trouble. This may be it. You two take the front stairs, since you have it mined. H. and I will go out the back. The super is under duress. He's with bad company, so do your thing."

"It can't be Palmer, or the super would have suggested so. How the devil could he get anyone to work for him?" Joe was talking aloud, but mostly to himself as they raced down the back stairs.

Henry Major had just passed his 58th birthday. He had been born in this house and followed in his father's footsteps. He was not an ambitious man, but he did his job well. His wife had died shortly after his father, just about seven years ago. He elected then to remain alone and spend his life superintending the building. Joe knew his small basement apartment well, as he had spent an occasional evening playing chess with Henry. Henry was on the slight side, his drawn leathery face seemed to process a permanent smile that went with his good nature. His clothes, though second hand, were always clean and pressed.

The basement was divided into three areas. The super's apartment occupied two of the three areas and had an exit beneath the front steps. The rear exit was adjacent to the back stairs. It contained the oil burner furnace and hot water heater, dumbwaiter, and storage bins. When they entered, they found the large room empty. A dozen boxes were attached about the walls, just above ground level. Each had a timer set for the same time and a switch set in the off position. Heather whispered to Joe. "He's still placing them."

Joe nodded. As they approached the apartment door, it opened and a woman appeared. She barely had time to be startled when she saw Heather's fist coming. It landed flush on her nose, and she dropped.

"My turn," she said to Joe.

Frank and Darin came in through the front door. The super's eyes were covered and he lay on his back, knees up, his hands cuffed with a plastic tie. The wall around the room supported more boxes. The clocks were set and ticking. They ignored the two victims until they had disarmed the explosives. While Frank untied the super, Darin removed the explosives and stacked them in a neat pile. Joe dampened a towel from the bathroom to contain the blood flowing from Heather's victim. The lady sat with her back against the wall. Her hands covered her nose. She was well proportioned, firm muscles, black short hair and dark complexion that suggested Spanish, Mexican or Portuguese. She wore a uniform of material that failed to hide her full breasts or generous hips. Joe handed her the towel to clean the blood from her face. She looked at him with hatred in her eyes.

"Hey, lady, I didn't hit you," Joe protested.

"Now then, whoever you are, tell us all about it or I'm going to make a Van Gogh out of you, one ear at a time. If you don't believe me, try me," Heather said. "Let's begin with names. Yours first. Now!"

The woman said nothing, just watched the towel turn red. With a swift movement Heather grasped the woman's ears and pulled them, hard. "Now, or I'll give a quick jerk." There was a scream of pain.

"Stop, please! Stop. I'll tell. It was a man named Potter. He..."

"First your name."

"I'm Frances Hurtel. I'm a hooker now, but I served in the army, Ordnance. Potter hired me for the night. He said it was worth 50 thousand dollars if I did the job and could get hold of the stuff to do it. He wanted the whole building to come down at one time, no questions asked. I could do a lot on that kind of money."

"Where did you get that amount of plastic?" Heather asked.

"From a sergeant friend I do tricks with now and then. He's maintenance at the local arsenal. Potter wanted some heavy stuff—a rocket launcher, that sort of thing. All I could get was the stuff here, honest."

"His name—the sergeant!" Heather's hand started toward the woman's ears again.

"Murphy, Sergeant George Murphy! Please, that's it!"

"Not quite. Tell us now about 'Potter'. Where is he waiting for you? How are you to contact him? When are you to be paid, and how?"

"He said he'd be close enough to see the implosion and when he did, he'd call me. Potter is a slight man, neatly dressed, looks like a salesman. Pale complexion and bad teeth. I always look at men's teeth. He needs dental work. He likes highly polished shoes."

"Did he specify the time, or did he leave that up to you?"

"No. I did that. I figured most people would still be at work, and the place would be quiet. Four o'clock was my choice."

"I see you're dressed as a meter reader. Was that your idea as well?"

"No, that was his. He wanted me to look like a man. May I get to a hospital now? My nose will have to be set. Where did you learn to punch like that? Were you in the army?"

Heather ignored her questions and looked at Joe. "I'll call Karp and tell him about Sergeant Murphy. He can make arrangements to take care of our friend, here. You want to question her, Joe?"

"Yes. Now, Ms. Hurtel, the sooner we get done, the sooner you'll get attention, so please don't ask questions or avoid ours. Understand?"

She looked at Joe strangely, in a way that he didn't understand. She softly said, "I understand." She saw him as someone most desirable.

"When you last saw your Mr. Potter, was that at your place or his?"

"He was eating at a Pancake House alone when I spotted him. I asked if I could share his table. He didn't mind, so I did. I propositioned him, and he said he was interested. He asked me right off what I did, and I told him about my army hitch and what I did there. He bought my meal and we went to my place. He bought my time for the whole day and night. Paid up front. He spent most of the time questioning me about the army and my connections. He showed me a lot of money and proposed this project. Hell, he was a nice little fellow, and that kind of money—maybe I could find a man like you and, well..."

"Did you see him anywhere other than your place?"

"No, and he said nothing at any time about himself. Well, except once he said something like I was the first woman he'd had in over two years. It could be, because he made up for lost time."

By the time Joe finished, he knew a lot about Palmer: his shaving habits, which leg he put into his trousers first, how he cleaned his fingernails, the side of the bed he preferred. We all have our own idiosyncrasies, and Palmer certainly had his. Joe wanted to be able to recognize Palmer under any conditions—from the back or side, standing or sitting—and this woman presented his first opportunity.

Heather returned from phoning Karp and asked Joe, "You about finished? Frank and Darin have all the plastic neatly packed in the canvas bag she brought it in. A van will arrive soon in the alley and pull into the carport."

"Yes, Frances should be attended to. I feel she's answered about everything. Have you anything to add, Ms. Hurtel?"

"Only, why didn't I meet you at the Pancake House instead of Potter?"

Joe smiled, "In a way you did."

***

Henry, the super, was shaken by the activity and horrified that his building was so close to falling in on him, that a woman could do such a thing, and that he could have let such a person in his home after being warned. Heather comforted him while extracting his promise of silence until the affair was concluded. They didn't want to stir up the neighborhood any more than need be. He marveled at Heather's laying out that tough woman who had hog-tied him so easily. He liked to think of her fist spreading that bitch's nose flat. That made everything right. It wouldn't be so easy for her to pick up a John from now on.

Joe exchanged a few words with Henry, promising a chess game soon, and told Heather that he was going out for a bike ride about the neighborhood. He asked her to wind things up and told her he'd see them all in the studio in an hour.

Then he ran up the back steps to the studio and changed into his bicycling outfit, adding a ski mask under his helmet. In the carport he unlocked a cabinet that held a pair of racing bikes. It was a half block before the chill left him and his muscles warmed as he sped down and up the streets. It felt good to ride again. Little escaped him. He coasted at times, sitting erect with his arms folded across his chest. No one paid attention to him. He was just another health nut who didn't recognize the season.

It was a minute after four when he approached a bus stop near a subway entrance and saw his man sitting on a bench. Joe was on the far side of the street however, and the traffic didn't permit him to cross. He spun the bike around and pedaled to the intersection, hoping to catch the light green. As he reached it, it turned red. The bench was no longer in sight, nor was his quarry. The caution yellow appeared across the intersection, and Joe put his full weight on the upper pedal as the green showed. The bike jumped forward and arrived at the bench within seconds. It was empty. A bus had just pulled out, as had a taxi. A dozen or so people disappeared into the subway entrance. Joe stood tall on the pedals, but saw no one who interested him.

***

Joe returned just as a van pulled out of the carport. Frank and Darin watched it leave as he rode up.

"Well, any luck?" Darin asked.

"I saw him, but the traffic prevented me from reaching him! He has the lives of a cat. But I saw him."

"Maybe it was best you didn't get closer this time. How would you stop him without weapons?" Frank asked.

"I don't know. I just would, somehow. My adrenaline was flowing. I don't think he saw me. The last thing he'd expect would be a bike rider. It was just after four, and no cloud of dust was rising from this direction. He knew he'd lost again, and he wanted to get off the street quickly."

"Think he'll give up, or come after you himself? I thought he'd come shooting by now. Think he's afraid?" Frank asked.

"Afraid not. He wants to savor his kill and the odds would be against him for that just yet. It may come to that if his funds run out. Our best bet now is to get to Sergeant George Murphy and hope Palmer will make contact with him directly. I'll call Karp and ask him to lay off for a few days. You two set something up that may bring the Sergeant and Palmer together. Take my car, and hurry. If I were Palmer, I'd call Murphy soon. Keep in touch. I have to call D.C."

***

The superintendent sat on the edge of his bed, head in hands. He was still in shock and disbelief that a woman could overpower him. He considered himself to be in good shape and rather strong. Perhaps it was because she tricked him, catching him off guard. She handed him her canvas sack, weighted down with high explosives and then kicked him in the shins. When he fell in pain, she helped him up and all but carried him to his bed, where she tied him up so easily. Heather comforted his wounded pride with words and his bruised shins with ice compresses. She then wiped up the blood-splattered floor against his protest. She insisted that he remain calm and rest. There was nothing he could do.

"I'm grateful, Mrs. Jensen. Just tell me, when did you learn to punch like that?"

"Oh, that. Joe taught me just the other day."

"Nothing surprises me about him, but you, you don't look the...I mean, er..."

"I understand, Henry. Now give yourself a couple more hours before you try walking."

To himself Henry said, "What I'd give to have such a wife. Maybe I'd better look around." Half aloud he said, "You don't have a sister, do you?"

Heather smiled a sisterly smile and said, "I'll leave you now and look for Joe. We'll look in on you later and thank you for all you've done for us."

"I don't understand. It's you who have..." His words were lost. Heather stepped out of the back door in time to see Joe coming in, still wearing his helmet.

"So you went cycling without me? Any luck?"

"I saw him. Would you believe—if it weren't for the traffic I would have had him. Thirty seconds. I would have had my hands on the rascal."

"Let's go upstairs and you can tell me about it," Heather said, leading the way.

"I must call Karp and have him hold off a day or two on picking up the Sergeant at the armory. I asked Frank and Darin to visit with him."

"That sounds promising," Heather said. "When you finish talking to Karp, we should call Robert and tell him what's going on. I want to know if he's popped the question to his lady, Kathryn, yet."

***

Chief Warrant Officer MacElheney was sharp and precise. "Gentlemen, what can I do for you?"

Frank and Darin felt they should salute. This fellow was right out of the book. Light reflected from polished buttons and shoe leather. His clean shaven face, like those used in recruiting posters, was strong as if chiseled from stone. His shoulders were broad, and the hand he extended was firm. The voice was warm. "Sit down. I've had word from Karp. My time and service are yours without question."

"We appreciate your help. We want to have Sergeant George Murphy give us his full attention for a day or two—not to take him away from his duties but to understand our position over him without his knowing just who we are," Darin said.

"He's yours. When do you want to see him?"

"Now, if possible."

The Chief picked up the phone and punched a few buttons. "You want him here or at the armory shed?"

"There."

The Chief spoke a few orders that no one would hesitate to obey. "You've got him. The corporal will drive you while you're on the base. Anything I can do, call. Pleasure to meet you, gentlemen." He saluted and offered his hand.

***

The armory shed was windowless, its gray steel walls were not welcoming. A simple green button seemed out of scale for the size of the door. A camera lens covered the present visitors. Darin smiled at the lens as he pressed the button. A buzzer sounded releasing the lock permitting access into the warehouse of weapons for destruction.

Sergeant George Murphy was pure army: rugged, square jawed, broad shouldered, with blonde cropped hair, neatly brushed, that glistened from brilliantine, and brass buttons as highly polished as were his shoes. A broken nose gave evidence that his temper paid a price. His hoarse voice spoke with authority. After greetings were exchanged, he asked.

"I don't understand what I can do for you fellows. Civilians have no right being here." The sergeant's voice showed his doubt.

It didn't help when Frank said, "Did your chief speak to you a moment ago?"

"Yes, but I thought I was going to see some braid."

"How much do you want to see, Sergeant? We may not wear it, but believe me, we have it, and more. Much more!" Frank said.

Darin shook his head and that was enough for the sergeant.

"We want to check your inventory of plastic and time fuses to begin with. We have a full written confession from an ex bed-companion of yours, Frances Hurtel, ex-PFC Hurtel." Frank's voice was calm, matter of fact.

"Good God! I told that bitch whore it would mean trouble. But she said no way. She wanted heavy stuff for some guy named Potter, who was throwing money around. Now I suppose my ass is cooked. What did they do with the damn stuff?" He paled. Then anger took over and he reddened.

Darin stepped toward the sergeant, "Sit down and listen good. I assume you haven't met or spoken to this Potter fellow, right? OK, then. We think that he will call or get in touch with you somehow, and this is what you're going to do—that is, if you want to save your ass. You're going to be bugged from now on. You are going to sleep with a bug. You'll hear from Potter or someone working for him. You're to play it cozy. Hard to get, but gettable, understand?

"Yes, sir."

"Good. Make your sale. Promise anything. We'll be listening in and keeping our distance, but eyeing you until this is over. Now here is the script for you." Darin and Frank spoke for another hour. As they were about to leave, the phone rang.

"Sergeant Murphy. Yes sir, yes, yes. When? Where? No problem. Frances said you were good for the money. No, I haven't. She only calls when she wants something. No, I have no idea. If she calls, I'll tell her. OK, till then." He hung up and asked, "How the hell did you know he'd call, and so soon?"

"That's part of our job. So now let's go over it."

The sergeant was used to giving orders, not taking them, especially from civilians. He didn't like or understand these men who used only their first names. But they had him over the barrel and his ass was in a sling. He could only hope that if he cooperated, somehow they could save his hide. The next time he saw that damn whore, Hurtel... She was responsible for getting him in this mess.

***

"What's the news from Robert?" Joe asked Heather. "Did he propose?"

"Not yet. He seems to think it has to be a very special occasion. Private, romantic setting, proper music with flowers, with all the icing on the cake. He can't hear me when I tell him that none of that stuff is important. The only thing a girl wants to hear is the four words. If she's ready, she'll let you know. Maybe not in so many words, but you'll know when. He was ready last night, he thought. He rehearsed before a mirror and choked with laughter at how ridiculous he looked. Joe did you feel foolish when you...?"

"I don't think so. But then, I'm in the habit of expressing myself. I think that Robert, with his law background, is more frightened to make a lifetime commitment. He's thinking of loopholes. Traditionally, in our family a commitment is for life. We believe in honor and all the values that most today couldn't care less about. Nevertheless Robert will come through. Kathryn will know and wait, and he's worth waiting for. I'll bet she'll propose to him, and he won't even know when it happens."

"Otherwise all is quiet in D.C.," Heather continued. "They've filled in the escape tunnel at the Speaker's house and sealed the second basement for good. The house has been up for sale, but so far there's been no interest. I made his day, telling him what's happened here."

Then Heather asked how long Joe thought it would be before they could fly to Dallas to see the property he'd described.

"I have a large aerial photo of the place in the drafting drawers," Joe said.

"You've been holding out on me."

"No, just waiting for the proper moment."

"You Jensen boys are alike. Always waiting for the right moment," she said, following Joe to the file drawers.

Joe removed a 24 x 30 inch black and white aerial photo from the bottom drawer and laid it face up on his drawing table.

"Wow! Joe, you own such a place and didn't even tell me. You're really something!" She kissed him full, long, and hard. "What other secrets are you keeping from me?'

"None for the moment," he said.

"You damn tease. But this is enough for many dreams. What a place to bring up a family. Shall we build a house with that in mind?"

"That's up to you, but right now, we must concentrate on Palmer. Think you can do that for a few more days? Now we have to wait for Frank and Darin to report on their results with the good sergeant."

***

Heather was examining the aerial map through a magnifying glass, inch by inch. Joe was sitting in his studio facing the toned linen surface of the canvas that awaited his brush. His thoughts were not on the composition to be established, but on Palmer, who was interfering with his time to create. He sensed that he had reached the inner workings of his adversary's mind and could anticipate his next move. Palmer had been frustrated on every attempt and now must perform himself. He was a back-shooter, relying on his wits, planning, and the skills of others to perform while he sought the safety of nearby shadows. His size and lack of physical prowess all but demanded he operate that way. His lack of conscience, destroying life if it got in his way, served as his strength. His fear of being harmed made him most cautious. He was like a hunter sitting in the safety of a blind, waiting for his prey to appear and offer him a clear shot for his trophy. Palmer had paid dearly in his failed attempts, both in money and in connections. Running low on both would require him either to give up or to have a go at it himself, which was most likely. To do so would require a weapon that would keep him out of reach while still being destructive enough to do the job. That would require knowing when his target was in position. How would he gain such knowledge without exposing himself?

His thoughts were interrupted by the arrival of Frank and Darin.

"Sorry if this is a bad time to disturb you, Joe. Our visit with the sergeant went too well for us to wait," Frank said.

"No problem, just meditating about our friend Palmer. Let's have coffee and hear what you learned from Sergeant Murphy," Joe suggested.

"What's that aerial photo that's put Heather in another world?" Darin asked.

"We'll share that with you later. Nothing to do with Palmer. H., you should join us. I guess I should put that photo up till we resolve the problem at hand."

"I know, love. You're a dream-maker. Let's find a way to wind this thing up and go on to happier pursuits. I'll make the coffee and see what tidbits are about."

"Come now, you really have us intrigued. What's this about?"

"Not now. If I open the subject—well, it will just have to wait. Tell us about the sergeant."

"OK. If you won't, you won't. Our sergeant was seduced, so he said, into selling the plastic explosives." Frank related the visit and phone call from Palmer and their scheduled meeting. He said they'd told the sergeant to promise Palmer/Potter anything he wanted, but to make him pay up front, as much as he could squeeze from him.

"Good, very good. That's more than we could have hoped for. You feel sure we can depend on the sergeant to cooperate?" Joe asked.

"Yes, unless he deserts. His future depends on it, and he knows that. Hope you agree. We thought it best to let him know the cost if he doesn't cooperate. We promised him nothing if he did. He knows we'll be listening in from a distance. Thought it best that he wear no bug for the meeting itself. Palmer is too smart and suspicious. A couple of Karp's new telescopic sound devices should do it, if we can keep within a hundred yards."

"Sounds good to me, Frank. You agree, H.?"

Heather poured the coffee. "I see no problems," she said.

"In the meantime, we'll have the sergeant bugged until the time of the meeting. This is more for psychological reasons, to keep him in line," Darin added.

"So where and when are they going to meet?"

"The sergeant is to be at a public phone in the Metropolitan Art Museum at 4 p.m. tomorrow for instructions. Karp's men will have bugged each phone by that time. We'll plant a homing button on the sergeant and follow from a block or two away. If we lose him—God forbid—we'll see him at the post."

"Darin, I hope you're right. I'd like to come face to face with Palmer, but if I can't, I have a trick or two up my sleeve that just might resolve our problem. In the meantime, I'll make a few calls, and you fellows keep the sergeant honest." Joe could feel the adrenaline flowing. For the first time since he started, he felt the pulse of Palmer.

"H., perhaps before long we can both dream of a new home."

***

Sergeant Murphy felt alone. His small office no longer offered the security it had for the past years. The comfort that Frances had offered from time to time to satisfy his urges was hardly worth the price he now had to pay. He loved the army. It was family, and all his friends were here. He swore to himself, at himself. At best he would lose his stripes. At worst, he'd get a dishonorable discharge and prison. And now he must do the bidding of outsiders. Well, so be it. If he must, he would, if it would help his cause. But first he'd see what Potter would offer. If it was enough, he could disappear and set himself up elsewhere. He would wait and see. His phone was tapped and he was wired. He felt an unseen presence at all times. It wouldn't be easy to escape—he'd have to leave everything behind and just vanish. That wouldn't be easy. Deserting the army was never easy.

***

In a commercial hotel in mid-Manhattan Palmer sat at a small desk studying a group of 8 x 10 glossy prints , still photos that had been enlarged from the video tape shot from the helicopter. A detailed map of Queens lay on the floor. A green circle encompassed several blocks around the building that housed Joe Jensen's studio. Several orange lines fanned out from it, stopping at various distances. Each line was marked with a number indicating the distance from point A (the studio) to B (placement of the weapon). A pad of pink paper held notes showing various times. Heavily underlined was 5:45 a.m.

He leaned back, rubbing his tired eyes, and smiled. It was all but done. He had a mental picture of a rocket falling into the center of the roof, penetrating the studio itself and exploding, turning the whole floor into instant ash. He laughed aloud to the empty room. "You smart bastard, I'll soon have you. Then I'll return to Paris and celebrate."

All he needed now was to contact Sergeant Murphy and have him deliver a launcher and a couple of rockets. It was about time to get himself together and get to the Metropolitan Museum. He knew Murphy would become nervous if he was kept waiting too long.

The idea of meeting the sergeant in the great hall of the largest treasure house of art in the Western hemisphere appealed to Palmer, and he chose the simple disguise of an artist. He wore heavy, deep brown corduroy trousers, tennis shoes, a turtleneck sweater, a denim jacket, and a paint-stained hat. He was impressed by the grandiose Fifth Avenue facade as he mounted the four tiers of marble steps. It was incredible to him that so many people had an interest in art. For the most part they looked happy and excited. As he passed through the gate, a guard looked at him and nodded a welcome. He thinks I'm a stupid painter, Palmer mused. The idiot. What's so special about painters? They paint things that have nothing to do with anything.

A bank of phones was just off to the right. A soldier was standing by the last phone glancing at his watch, then staring at the crowds as they entered and left. He glanced at Palmer and dismissed him. At one minute to four, the sergeant dropped a coin into the box and punched the numbers.

At the first ring Palmer picked up the phone at the other end of the row and said, "Potter here."

"Murphy," a nervous voice said.

"Sergeant, listen well. I'll say this once only. I want a launcher and two high-explosive rockets. How much?"

"Twenty-five G's on delivery."

"OK, I agree. Put the items in a crate. Mark it 'art work' and have it at The Club Boathouse, Flushing Bay, tomorrow at 7 a.m. sharp." Palmer hung up and walked slowly toward the sergeant.

The sergeant hung up and turned to walk away when he bumped into a painter. "Sorry," he mumbled as he walked by.

Frank was leaning against the brass rail on the upper steps of the museum when Darin joined him.

"See Palmer?"

"No. Too many people or a hell of a disguise."

"The sergeant?" Darin asked.

"At the bus stop. See him?"

"Yeah. I'll go back in and look around. May be lucky. We'll give it an hour."

As Darin walked past, the artist was looking at a bulletin board that announced the new acquisitions to the permanent collection. Listed on it was the name Joe Jensen, oil on canvas, 48 x 60 inches, titled: Interior, Warm Light. The artist joined a group of students who were making their way to the galleries.

***

As Sergeant Murphy approached his office he noticed a young man out of uniform sitting at his desk. It would be good to chew out someone. He needed to blow off steam. He was puffed up, ready, when a calm voice said with authority, "You talked to Potter, now talk to me."

"Who will I be talking to then?"

"I'm with Frank and Darin. Your conversation was recorded and relayed to me. I'm sure you have little idea who Potter is or what he has done, much less what he plans to do."

"For God's sake, let me in on something."

"All you need to know, Sergeant, is that you're dealing with a ruthless killer, one who kills without conscience or hesitation. You're going to deliver the weapon he wants and try to collect your money. You'll be wearing a flack jacket and a steel head-band painted to match exactly your flesh color. Your new friend likes to place his shots between the eyes. We'll try to cover you."

"Try to cover me!?! What the hell does that mean!?! You trying to scare me? Well, you have."

"Calm down. Potter is a cautious man, but I don't think he's aware of what we know. So be the man you think you are. Remember, this is your own private war. You brought yourself into it."

"There must be a better way to get this guy."

"It's all set up, so play your part well and it may save both you and your lady friend. The weapons crate is being prepared for you to deliver as scheduled. Stay within the post in the meantime."

"Well, at least tell me who the hell you guys are. You seem to take over everything and give nothing."

"What you don't know, Sergeant, can't hurt either you or us. Relax and enjoy it."

As Joe left, he heard the sergeant mutter. "Relax and enjoy it, bull!"

***

A light snow began to fall, only to disappear as it touched the warm ground. The Club Boathouse was closed for the season. A single, bare, sixty watt lightbulb flickered above its side door. The bay was still reflecting warm, distant light like lines drawn on the surface. Now and then indistinguishable voices shouted orders from nowhere. It was seven o'clock when the headlights approached the pier by the boathouse. A small pickup stopped and cut off its motor. Two long minutes went by before the stillness was broken.

"Bring the crate to the edge of the wall."

The truck door squeaked open and the sergeant stepped out, looking neither right nor left. He removed the crate from the back of the truck and carried it to the wall. He looked over to see a pair of hands reaching up to take it.

"My money first, then your damned weapon."

"It's in the envelope, just out of your reach," the voice below said. "Now the crate."

The sergeant pushed the crate into the waiting hands and peered over to see a dark form below in a small speed boat. He pulled back and reached for the envelope, only to see it fly into the air as the boat roared to life. The sergeant jumped up cursing when he felt a sudden sharp pain. Then everything went dark. Shots rang out from the pier as strong beams of light crossed the now-choppy surface, seeking the small boat's wake. The little boat disappeared behind a dredging barge but reappeared a moment later, only to erupt into flames. Soon all was silent except for the faint sound of music from far away. The surface of the water became smooth again, and the white lines of light returned to unbroken shapes.

Night glasses were focused on the activity from a small dory that supported an electrically driven motor. Heather held the glasses steady as she watched a figure place the crate on a platform, then leap from the small speed boat. The throttle was pushed wide open, and the boat roared off to its fiery destruction moments later. The figure loaded the crate into a second boat that was powered with the same kind of motor. The boat kept the dredge barge between itself and the shore and soon disappeared into the night. "Think you're clever, don't you, Mr. Palmer," Heather spoke to the disappearing boat.

***

"Wake up, Sergeant. Your Irish temper almost got you killed, but over all, you did well," Frank said, slapping Murphy's face. "See, you are a good soldier after all. The envelope was filled with newspaper. He had a fish line attached to it to sucker you into standing up so that he could shoot you right between the eyes. Almost wish we could let him know. You hear me, Sergeant?"

"Yes, I hear you. My head! What an ache." His voice drifted off as his eyes closed again.

"Well, it looks like Palmer did it again. He must think he's invincible. That was quite an escape. Joe, I could have picked him off with a 30-30."

"No doubt you could, H., but I think it would be neater if he pulled the trigger himself. If we'd done it the first time, it would have saved several lives, but for the most part, they were his own people."

"May I suggest we continue this over some pasta. My treat," Darin said.

"I go for that, partner. I know just the Mom and Pop place. Heather? Joe? OK, let's loosen our belts."

"I don't want to be a spoil sport, but remember we still may have to move fast. Besides, if all goes well, we may have to have the most perfect breakfast at the B and B tomorrow. Tonight we spend on the roof under a blanket of low-hanging clouds filled with snow."

***

Palmer understood most men's weaknesses, but Sergeant Murphy had given him a moment of doubt. Murphy was married to the army. It was the major factor in his life, and for Palmer's purposes he could not be fully trusted. His sexual drive might be understood, but it appeared he'd never betray a trust for money. Murphy didn't seem overbright, though, and might be just the one to get the weapon Palmer needed.

Palmer assumed a trap would be laid, but he would again outwit them if indeed the sergeant's morality got the better of him. Either way, he would get his weapon and the sergeant would get his reward for betraying his country.

So Joe Jensen had a painting in the Metropolitan Museum. Well, he would make Joe famous. After all, dead painters are worth more than live ones. The thought pleased him.

Palmer had paddled the small boat close to the wall, being careful not to splash or stir the surface. As the small truck's headlights crossed the wall he had pulled up and sat in silence until he heard the car door open. After he reached up and placed an envelope with a fish line firmly glued at a corner on top, he had asked the sergeant to bring the crate to the edge, waving his hands to guide him. Then, he had jerked the fish line, making the envelope fly from Murphy's grasping hands. As the speed boat coughed into life, and gained speed, Palmer turned, knowing the sergeant would curse him, making a perfect target. His shot was lost in the roar of motor. "A third eye for you, friend." His words, too, were lost. His plan worked as he knew it would. He did not hear or see the gun flashes that followed him.

***

It was after midnight when Palmer removed the last screw from the crate. It had not been easy for so slight a man to maneuver the heavy wooden crate up three flights of stairs to his recently rented apartment. He had chosen it carefully. It was just eight blocks from his target. He told the agent that his family would be following with the van containing their household furnishings in a few days. A deposit was good enough for him to acquire a set of keys. He had set up a tripod on the roof that could support a launcher at the exact elevation and direction to deliver its payload to the center of his target. The second missile would follow within 30 seconds.

The hours spent with the photos and maps, calculating the distance and the projection of the missile's flight, would soon pay off. No longer would he have to depend on someone else to pull the trigger.

Ever so gently he removed the top of the crate. Tears flooded his eyes as he looked at the beautiful instrument that at long last would bring death to his nemesis. As he had once killed the father, Senator Ralph Jensen, now he would kill the painter son. He stroked the long metal surface of the launcher as if were a pet. Then he removed one of the rockets and examined it closely. He held it in both hands, turning it slowly. It felt right and looked as if it had not been tampered with. Palmer was excited. He could feel his heart pound. He laughed aloud. All he had left to do was to set it up on the roof.

***

"So now we set ourselves up on the roof for the night. Is this necessary, Joe?" Heather asked.

"Relax, H., just relax. Pretend you're in the mountains, surrounded by sweet-smelling tall timber at the edge of a placid lake, in a sleeping bag, listening to night noises. Or think of exploring our new home site."

"You win. I'll go quietly."

"Shall we pass the time with a few hands of bridge?" Frank suggested.

"First let's get ourselves comfortable and hope everything goes as planned. Palmer may suspect the missiles were tampered with. I may be relying on his ego too much. It took a long time to set him up to pull the trigger himself. An hour or two should prove the plan one way or another, so let's take a thermos of hot coffee and get ourselves on the roof."

***

Palmer made the final adjustments to assure the exact angle and direction required for the launcher to deliver the missile that would bring his long quest to its proper end. He placed heavy weights on the feet of the tripod to secure it from any unforeseen movement that might change its carefully calibrated aim.

He envisioned the night sky turning red over the senator's son studio, filling the air with bits of paintings and painter. A smile widened across his face at the thought.

He glanced at his watch. It showed three minutes to three. Time to die, he said aloud as his finger released the trigger mechanism. Horrified realization erased his smile. He failed to check the interior of the barrel of the launcher.

***

A little before three the sky lit up with a bright flash of white-yellow, then turned the low-hanging cloud cover a deep orange-red. As Joe counted, the sound of the explosion followed. "Southeast, about eight blocks away. Let's go!"

***

They turned away in silence to return to the studio while the firemen were still winding up the tangled mess of hoses and the fire chief barked orders. His report would be echoed in the morning press: "Man blown up while experimenting with rocket on roof of apartment in Queens early this morning. No other injuries. See details on page 16." On page 16 the bold type to continue the story read: "To kill one's self."

***

As they prepared for bed, Heather asked, "When do we go to Texas?"

"Would you believe I have tickets for this evening?"

The end.